SOULWORK

Connecting with the Universe and your Spiritual
Path to Find your True Purpose in Life

ELIZABETH RADCLIFFE

Design and Distribution by Bublish, Inc.

ISBN: 978-1-647044-07-7 (Paperback)
ISBN: 978-1-647044-06-0 (EBook)

CONTENTS

"Every generation interprets Trickster anew."
—*Paul Radin*

(Radcliffe, 2021, quoting Hyde,
1998, quoting Radin, 1956)

This book is dedicated to all the Guides and Tricksters in my life,
both seen and unseen,
but especially V & A.

To my parents, who have always been there for me.

And to my dear friend Maggie, who captured with a cover image
both earthy and ethereal the layered beauty of doing our Soulwork.
You can find more of her art at
www.maggierubinart.com

AN INVITATION TO DANCE

(A story that came to me, from Anansi, while writing about Trickster)

Once, the Sky God had a beautiful tapestry.
It was so intricate and colorful the Great Divine Being
loved nothing more than to contemplate it all day.

Because the Sky God kept his tapestry locked away
and would never let anyone look at it,
Anansi, the spider trickster, plotted to steal it.

However,
since he could never lift anything so heavy as the enormous tapestry,
Anansi decided to take it apart,
move it thread by thread,
and re-weave it somewhere else.

One morning, when the Sky God went to view his
beloved tapestry, he did not see it on the wall.
Instead,
he found a pile of mixed-up threads on the floor
and noticed a small, round mound moving underneath.
It was Anansi.

"Anansi!" The Sky God thundered; the air charged with his anger.
"Yes, Father?" came the meek, muffled reply.
"What have you done to my beautiful tapestry?"
"Um…" Anansi cleared his throat. "I was making a gift for you,
but you interrupted me before it was ready."

"You destroyed my tapestry as a *gift?*" the Sky God asked
incredulously, sure that this was one of Anansi's tricks.

Anansi looked at the pile of threads in quiet consideration.

Then, struck by inspiration, he said softly,
"Yes, my father. This tapestry is so boring and still, it may be
beautiful, but it never does anything but sit here on this wall.
I was planning to give each of the humans one
of the threads and teach them to dance.
As they all move together through life, they will re-weave your tapestry.
When the dance is finally done, you will have
your beloved wall-hanging back."

The Sky God looked at the pile of threads and thought for a long while.
"You may do this," he finally agreed.

So it was that Anansi began his role in our lives,
giving us our threads and teaching us to dance.

As the Sky God watched us weave the beautiful patterns
of our hearts into color and motion and sound,
he realized he would never quite have his beloved tapestry back.

In its place, he had something much better:
a constantly changing ensemble that turned the
light of his initial creation into a rainbow.

He was so pleased with his gift that he gave one to Anansi in return.
"Anansi," he said,
"from now on, you will always be a weaver;
a weaver of webs,
a weaver of threads,
a weaver of stories."

An Opening

Approaching the Aperture

Most of us have had at least one moment in our lives that ripped a hole in our understanding of reality. Maybe you've experienced an odd coincidence or had a wish unexpectedly granted. Maybe you've encountered a spiritual practice—meditation, yoga, acupuncture, or a martial art—that changed your orientation to the world. Or, perhaps, your introduction to spirituality sprouted in more somber soil, a small stalk of hope rising out of the loam of sadness and loss. Twenty-five years ago, my own spiritual journey grew from roots just like these.

Shortly after my seventeenth birthday, an extracurricular Tai Chi class led by a beloved, eclectic English teacher introduced me to my "chi"—the Chinese word for *breath* and, also, life-force energy. Feeling the tingly, taffy-like sensation between my hands opened an entirely new way to experience my existence. Every night before bed, I would sit with my chi—which I'd started thinking of as, simply, *my energy*. As the internet age dawned, I had unknowingly begun a meditation practice before I had ever heard the word "meditation."

The following March, in an old church on the southern coast of England, a desperate plea scribbled on a pink paper fish served as my gateway to the Spiritual Path, our road to self-discovery and life purpose. But, I would not realize that until half a decade later.

A difficult breakup with a boyfriend that same summer yanked Cupid's arrow right out of my chest, leaving behind a raw and gaping wound. My heart dutifully pumped blood to the beat as it always had, though, leading me to wonder: if my heart, the physical organ, was fine, what was the *source* of my soreness? Why did I feel *pain* in my *chest*? A search for answers led me to the chakra system, an ancient organization of the body's energy centers.

Instead of running from the anguish, I dove in, allowing my heart to fully open as I meditated under the noon-day sun, unintentionally triggering a two-year experience of mystical bliss.

When my euphoria waned and the practicalities of life structured my days again, I began spontaneously "manifesting." Without conscious effort, whatever I wished for materialized before me, from meeting the man who would become my husband to getting a job at the company where I most wanted to work. Even small, seemingly meaningless things that I desired, a popcorn bowl I had my eye on, for example, dropped into my lap like magic.

And that was only the first five years.

On my early Path, I searched for a mentor or a book to explain what was happening to me. (I couldn't be the *only* person having such adventures.) But I could never really find either. At the time, I simply stumbled around, trying to make sense of what my world had become. My understanding of reality had changed so drastically, I felt uncomfortable even using the word.

When we wade into unknown territory, we want concrete data and hard evidence to chart our course through the tricky terrain. But, scientific investigation can lag behind real-world experience, and we *don't* have much research on the Spiritual Path to rely on. To safely pursue soul growth, we need to navigate the nebulous space between scientific understanding and blind faith.

Thus, I had to become the scientist of my own life: experimenting, collecting data, drawing conclusions, and then continuing to challenge the conclusions I'd already drawn. And while I never found a source that captured the whole of my experience, I did find reading material on mythology, pop culture physics, spirituality, intuition, and psychology, which lit my Path in their own way.

With this book, I attempt to knit together the threads of our spiritual engagement into one cohesive whole. Intuition, manifestation, and working with the unseen world are all pieces of our overall Relationship with the Universe, our Spiritual Path, and our Soulwork. This is the reference I would have wanted when I first tumbled, unsuspecting, into the *un*real world. The process described within is a structured—though unconventional—approach to life that demystifies the spiritual development process, helps you get out of your own way, and supports you in discovering why you are here on Earth.

WHAT MAKES ME THE EXPERT?

With what authority do I write this book? Any mainstream publisher worth their salt asks this question. Do I have an expansive CV of impressive credentials? Have I helped thousands of clients across years of professional practice? Do I have a social media platform with millions of followers to whom I can market my material?

I have none of those things.

What I do have, though, is two and a half decades of experience *doing* this work. And not *just* doing it, but balancing it with a full-time, demanding career, as a marital partner in a nearly twenty-year relationship, as a mom of two young children, and through an emotionally tumultuous divorce. Ironically, the very thing that would cause most publishers to turn their backs is what makes my book of *most value* to you: I'm ordinary. Soulwork didn't take over my life; it helped me create it. If you want to integrate spiritual development with living a practical, comfortable life, my years of practice doing just that provide valuable lessons from the trenches.

I am an ordinary person leading an *extraordinary* life—and if you aren't already, you could be, too.

Everyone starts somewhere. Right now, for example, you are starting this book. All journeys have a beginning, and while I am far from the beginning of my spiritual journey, I am at the beginning of sharing what I've learned with others.

Before my first child inched her way into this world, I read almost a dozen books about childbearing. Many were scientific and focused on the biology and technicalities of labor and delivery. Yet the one that provided me with the most helpful, applicable information about the *experience* of childbirth was *Diary of a Midwife*, by Julia van Olphen-Fehr, in which the author shares her stories of participating in home births in rural Virginia.

In like fashion, I've populated this book with my own stories of navigating my Spiritual Path and engaging with my Soulwork. I share them, hoping they offer some resonance and comfort as you walk your own Path.

Many teachers have advised me on my journey. Some I have worked with in person. Others I encountered only in books or other media. I owe most of the first decade of my Path work to the influence of Joseph Campbell's hallmark book *Hero with a Thousand Faces* and whatever VHS lectures of his I could find at my local library. Several other author-teachers who catalyzed my growth without us ever making eye contact are Huston Smith, Sharon Pearson, Gary Zukav, Lewis Hyde, Alberto Villoldo, and Carl Jung.

I feel a particular need, as well, to call out best-selling author and spiritual leader Sonia Choquette. I only found her work a dozen years after starting my own, but attending her workshops, participating in her online courses, and reading about her life validated, enhanced, and enriched the foundation I already had.

Before Sonia, I had only experienced my Relationship with the Universe through the lens of energy sensitivity and working with external signs from the Universe. Her teaching exercises helped me connect with my *internal* guidance system, my intuition, and introduced me to the idea of working with specific Guides rather than just the Universe-at-large. Many transformative epiphanies of my life surfaced because of her work. Although this book is born from my own personal journey, her impact can be felt strongly throughout.

HOW THIS BOOK WORKS

The first part of the book explores, in detail, the benefits of undertaking our Soulwork. We'll lay out the rules that structure the Relationship with the Universe and introduce a key guide on the Spiritual Path. I'll detail some "gear" that will aid us on our spiritual adventure and share a few last pieces of advice before embarkation. Peppered throughout the text are exercises designed to assist in processing the content. A dedicated notebook or sketchbook to record your thoughts would be a valuable companion for your adventure.

The second part of the book focuses on initiating contact with the Universe and connecting with our Spiritual Path. We'll cover strategies for quieting the mind, crafting a meditation practice, and developing energy sensitivity—three preliminary skills to help you find and navigate your Soulwork. Even if you have some experience with all of these, it's worth at least skimming this section. You may find some ideas that augment your current routine.

In the third part, we demonstrate how a Relationship with the Universe works, breaking down how to receive and interpret spiritual signs. We'll address some challenges specific to working with divine guidance. We'll also discuss guidelines for determining when you're receiving messages from the Universe (versus coincidence or your imagination), different mechanisms of communication, strategies for interpretation, and how to respond back to the Universe, cultivating an ongoing dialogue.

The book's final part covers navigating the Spiritual Path, revealing our Soulwork, and strategies to approach what we unearth. We'll distinguish the different phases of the Path, including Spiritual Testing and the Dark Night of the Soul. We'll propose exercises and ideas for finding the soul challenges specific to us. And, finally, we'll share techniques for healing our wounds and bringing our gifts into the world.

If you are new to the nebulous world of spiritual development, I hope this book, in whatever way appropriate, changes your life. Developing a Relationship with the Universe, walking the Spiritual Path, and engaging with my Soulwork changed mine forever. If you are already well on your way, I hope this book can provide any validation you need to celebrate what you have already accomplished or help wherever you may be struggling. So many books have been instrumental on my own Path in just such a way. Regardless of what brought you to this precipice, if you've come this far, there's a reason. There's something in this book for you.

PART 1

Crossing the Threshold

What to Know Before You Go

1

THE INVISIBLE WALL

Why Pursue Our Soulwork?

The Soul both does and does not want to do its Soulwork. On the one hand, there's nothing more rewarding than healing a deep wound or shining up a skill for display. On the other, Soulwork isn't always easy or fun. Even finding and bringing our talents into the world—something we all hope to do—can be long, painful, and fraught with anxiety.

On top of that, Soulwork often requires looking at pieces of ourselves that aren't wonderful, beautiful, and laudatory. We may keep awareness of these parts of our personality so far from our conscious minds that we no longer believe them to be within us. Instead, we project them onto others.

It's not my hidden feelings of inadequacy that are the issue; it's that you never seem satisfied with anything I do.

The problem is not that I'm self-conscious and vulnerable; it's that you always ask such rude and invasive questions!

Many of our ongoing internal and external struggles are a manifestation of wounds and fears we hide from ourselves. Thus, our engagement with the world ends up reinforcing those wounds instead of healing them.

After the birth of my first child, the rapport between myself and my then mother-in-law unexpectedly started to deteriorate. What had long been a supportive and caring relationship slid into one characterized by coldness, discomfort, and even tears. Sometimes mine. Sometimes hers. One night, as I breastfed my infant daughter after a particularly testy exchange, I applied some focused meditation to the problem. *Why is there so much animosity between us?* I wondered.

The answer, a piece of Soulwork, revealed itself during my meditation: I felt inadequate as a mother.

When my mother-in-law told stories about raising her three children while working a full-time job, I'd silently projected into those tales subtle rebukes of my mothering skills. I'd subconsciously taken my own fear—that I was not a capable mother—and overlaid it onto her. I saw it as *her* opinion of me rather than recognizing it as *my* opinion of *myself*. Underneath, though, my self-perception was to blame. In honesty, I could admit she had nothing to do with it. Her first grandchild had just been born—of course it would bring up memories of her own mothering experiences, and she would want to share them.

This realization brought on a wave of tears. Not only was I now facing my deep-seated feelings of inadequacy, but I also grappled with the recognition that I might be entirely to blame for the contentious turn our relationship had taken. And believe me—I really, *really* wanted it to be her fault. I was ready to walk with open arms into the sisterhood of suffering daughters-in-law. But no, it had to be me.

Discovering unsettling truths about ourselves is challenging, and even when we find the root of a problem, we don't always know how to solve it. Knowing may be "half" the battle, but we still have the remainder of the battle to fight, and now we're emotionally drained from the first half. At these low points of self-discovery, our Relationship with the Universe reminds us: when we're willing to take on our Soulwork, the Universe is always in our corner. The Spiritual Path, too, acts as a framework, providing supporting context to our travails. Together, they infuse us with the strength to pick our hearts up off the floor and forge ahead, trusting in a brighter future.

But wait! Facing uncomfortable parts of ourselves? Realizing we might bear some responsibility in many of the challenging things that happen to us? Piling "Soulwork" on top of a life already full of vocational work, family, and social responsibility? Who wants to do that?

Which raises the question: Why pursue our Soulwork at all? Why not remain content in a nice, peaceful ignorance?

CONNECTION AND MEANING

Soulwork helps us understand *why* things happen to us and how we have contributed to their presence in our lives. The more Soulwork we work through, the faster we comprehend challenges and can move obstacles out of our way. Rather than being bandied about on the waves of chance, we engage with existence through thoughtful experimentation, knowing the Universe supports our development.

I remember my life before I started this journey. Even though I had friends, romance, and a family who loved me, I still felt isolated—sometimes depressed—and occasionally even suicidal. I didn't understand any of these feelings, where they were coming from, or why I had them—I just did. I also felt that I should be "doing something," but I wasn't sure what. Failing to understand the *why* of my feelings only further contributed to my disappointment in myself.

From the first moment of feeling the magnetic pull of my energy between my palms, I knew I had connected to something beyond the boundaries of my own skin. Suddenly, my world felt fuller than it ever had before: full of life, full of color, full of purpose, and full of meaning. Lonely no longer, my link to the Universe lived within me always. As I wound my way—bit by bit, deeper and deeper into the self—incidents and accidents revealed my soul's wounds to me. With this newfound clarity, I could stop subconsciously suffering under the weight of those wounds and start doing something about them. Finding and working on my Soulwork was and is my true purpose in life—as I believe it is for all of us. It doesn't have to be our *only* purpose, but it's a great place to start!

HAPPINESS

When we connect with the Universe, walk our Spiritual Path, and engage with our Soulwork, we develop a solid core of inner joy.

In the summer of my sophomore year in high school, I signed up for a karate course. I actually only attended a single class. In it, the instructor introduced us to "horse stance." Like the posture of riding a horse, the position requires bending both knees in a deep squat so that the upper thighs become almost parallel to the floor. It lowers our center of gravity so that we're more stable and grounded. As we contend with more and more of our Soulwork, our happiness starts to mirror "horse stance": stabilizing and becoming more difficult to topple. We also find comfort and security in knowing we are doing the work we were born to do.

Is it possible to knock someone off balance if they're standing in "horse stance"? Yes. But when our joy is no longer *tied* to people, occupations, or other nouns, when bliss blossoms from within, it takes a 9.4 on the Richter scale to bring us down.

Did my divorce sweep me off my feet for sixty to ninety days? Yes, absolutely. Are there still moments of sadness in my life? Yes, of course. On an everyday basis, though, my Relationship with the Universe and the insight gained in doing my Soulwork allow me to easily reset and recharge. Drawing from a deep well of joy, love, and connection, we can manage high levels of stress without a discernible impact on our physical or emotional state.

Over my last twenty years of working in corporate America, I've had moments where I confessed to feeling "really stressed" about a particular project or situation, and my co-workers responded, "Well, you don't seem particularly stressed. I've seen stressed-out people, and that is not you." It makes me wonder why communicating stress requires high-performance-value drama. Can we not just trust people when they say they are stressed?

Amid one particularly challenging project, I told my boss, "Every day I come in like a rainbow and leave like a thundercloud—I would be happy if I could just end the day as a light drizzle." Working through some of my deepest Soulwork to date, I got there. In the process, I enriched my relationships with others on the team, found new growth opportunities, and improved my standing in the department overall.

As a token to commemorate the project's successful completion, a team member created a baseball-style collector's card with figures representing all of us on the core team. He used the character of Joy from the Pixar film *Inside Out* to characterize me. Although Joy goes through lots of anxiety and strain in the movie, she will always *be* Joy. That's who she is. I felt deeply honored to have been witnessed in such a way by another. My Spiritual Path journey and the strength of my Relationship with the Universe have made me the joyful person I am today. And so it can be for all of us.

RESILIENCE

Even when something *does* knock us off balance, the stability of our Relationship with the Universe, the deep sense of meaning in our lives, and our foundation of positivity enable us to bounce back faster.

We call this skill *resilience*—the ability to adapt to, recover from, and transform relative to negatively perceived events.

Despite the demise of my twenty-year romantic relationship, my twenty-three-year Relationship with the Universe still functioned perfectly. That solid core of support helped me realize, very early on, that I would find my feet again.

Even in maneuvering through my divorce, I operated from a place of joy and comfort much of the time. I know my own worth and value, even if my ex-husband did not. Because of my soul-work, that's not something I just tell myself—I embody it.

We might wonder, though, why the divorce happened at all? Shouldn't addressing our Soulwork help us prevent such disasters from occurring?

Yes and no.

The resilience we develop in working through our Soulwork allows us to honor others on their own journeys, even when their paths lead them in directions we wish they wouldn't go. Trying to prevent people from having their own journey helps no one and can lead to prolonged hurt all around. Even when, deep down, we think people might be making a mistake, the best we can do is share what we feel and respect their right to follow the path they choose. And who knows, we may find out that *we* were the ones who didn't see the whole picture. Sometimes the "bad" things that happen to us happen *for* us as well.

The Spiritual Path and the Relationship with the Universe provide a support structure that makes our Soulwork more manageable, accelerating the speed with which we can navigate challenges life throws our way. The more Soulwork we contend with, the more tools and experience we pick up for use in the next round. In actively approaching our Soulwork, we build our resilience for the unexpected events that threaten to upend our lives.

Support from the Universe may show up as guidance in a challenging situation. Support may show up as the Universe making sure we get the resources we need in times of strife. Support may show up in the zing of inspiration and clarity that comes when we least expect it.

Days after my then-husband confessed he wanted a divorce, I meditated in one of the chairs I had purchased just weeks before, with a hopeful heart, planning to turn a corner of our master bedroom into a gaming nook for the two of us. Tearfully, I beseeched my Guides, "Yes, I know you guys are here for me. I feel that. And I'm *so*, so grateful for your presence, but I need people—real, *live*, actual people right now."

And then, out of nowhere, invitations came pouring in…from people who weren't even aware of my marital strife. The next day, I received an e-vite to a ladies' night in the neighborhood we had moved into only four months before. Through a completely different avenue of my life, I was welcomed into a women's book club. I met several nice men through an online dating site and had five dates set up in less than a month with men who had themselves gone through divorces. Female friends who found out about the split connected me to *their* female friends who were further down the same road and could help me see a brighter future.

My parents offered to temporarily move in to help care for my two young daughters and provide some financial assistance. I gratefully took them up on that, and their presence immeasurably aided both my and my daughters' healing process. As had happened so many times before, I asked, and the Universe responded immediately. You want people? Okay, you got people.

Not all those invitations turned into lasting situations. And yet, that worked out perfectly, too. I had significant internal healing to do. An overly buzzing social calendar would have made that much more difficult. Those dates, for example, taught me that I was *far* from ready for a new romantic relationship—but they allowed me to meet others who had gone through the pain of divorce and were further along. They served a more important function as well: helping me see that I was still an attractive, engaging woman who could one day find romantic interest again.

The Universe provided exactly what I needed when I needed it most, surrounding me in a cocoon of love and support at the peak of vulnerability. This assistance is available to all of us, and this book provides a path to help you find it.

THE ABILITY TO ENACT DRAMATIC CHANGE AND CO-CREATE A BETTER LIFE

Once we understand how the Spiritual Path and our Relationship with the Universe works, our lives can radically change for the better with minimal effort on our part. I've co-created my marriage, my children, every career move I've made since college, and many more things besides. And each time it happens, there's always something magically effortless about the experience.

It's uncanny enough that even my atheist husband-at-the-time felt compelled to acknowledge it when I gushed about finding my dream job to a fellow mother at a preschool function.

"How long were you looking for a position?" she asked.

The question caught me off-guard, but my then-husband stepped in with a chuckle, "Beth doesn't look for jobs," he said, "jobs look for Beth."

A flattering thought, but not entirely accurate. Truthfully, after working through some torturous Soulwork, I had realized I needed a job change that allowed me to work from home more often and shift my hours. Directly following that epiphany, an opportunity matching those exact specifications appeared. I hadn't spent a minute searching for a position, but the opening had just become available; it certainly hadn't been *looking* for me.

When we feel stuck in our lives, it usually turns out that we are the blockers of the change we seek. The understanding we develop about how the Spiritual Path works can help us see that. The more practice we get, the more quickly we can flow into living our happiest, most fulfilling life.

Some years ago, I was gifted the opportunity to help a coworker with her own co-creation challenge. She and I had become casual friends over the years. On a coffee walk before work one morning, she confessed a hope to move out of state. Having initially moved to Chicago to spend more time near her birth family, she now missed her husband and grown children; she wanted to see them more often.

The only problem? Finding a job in her planned locale proved more elusive than she expected. As we conversed, I sensed that she had made finding a job in this new location a condition of moving rather than being fully committed in her heart to the move. It's understandable, of course; few of us want to move somewhere new without assurance we'll have the income to support us.

Because of the way the Universe works, though, *her fear of not finding a job was blocking her ability to make the move she wished for.*

Our Relationship with the Universe happens on an *energetic* level. For now, think of this as the Universe paying attention to her *emotions* rather than her mental criteria. From the Universe's perspective, her intentions were unclear. Did she *want* to move? Or was she *afraid* to move? Should the Universe respond to her fear and create more obstacles or to her desires and manifest a path forward?

"Do you really want to relocate?" I asked her.

She insisted that she did. We talked a bit about Spirituality, and she indicated that she, too, was a spiritual person—a Christian—and felt very connected with God.

"That's great!" I told her, knowing it would only take a slight tweak to resolve her issue. She already felt connected to the divine and was *open* to the idea of help from an unseen source.

"Since you already have faith," I advised, "my recommendation would be to really question, in your heart, whether you want to move. If you do, concentrate only on *that* desire in your heart. Make the decision that you are going to move no matter what. In fact, give yourself a date and commit that you're going to leave on that date, job or no. And then pray about it. Everything else will flow from that."

She appreciated my advice and agreed to try it. A few weeks later, she turned to me one morning flush with happy news; not only did she have one job offer in her desired location, but *two*. Even better, neither required her to leave the company. Both were great offers, and she was having difficulty choosing between them. What a great problem to have! She successfully transferred only a few months later.

The conversation with my coworker went much more smoothly than it might have with someone without any spiritual framework at all. Our internal beliefs around what is or isn't possible can act as a ceiling for our own experience.

We tell ourselves, "I can't have a job I love that pays me well, where I feel fulfilled, and I work with great people."

What can the Universe do with that? Fortunately, we don't have to believe that we *can* have those things to trigger life-changing help from the Universe. We just have to *stop sending the wrong message*.

The Universe can't remove the limitations we place on our own reality. If we transmit out *"I can't"* energy, the Universe will allow us to maintain that belief as long as we want. If it feels fake to replace "I can't" with "I can" (as it did for me), don't do that. Radiating inauthentic energy won't change your signal to the Universe because *you* don't really believe what you're transmitting.

Instead, switch from "I can't" to "I don't know." For example, next time you notice that you're telling yourself, "I can't have…" or "I can't expect…" or "It's impossible that…" stop, take a breath, and change it to "I don't know what's possible, but I'm not going to self-limit anymore." Can you feel the truth in that statement?

I can't stress enough that it doesn't matter what faith you belong to; this work is a *process,* not a religion. Even if you don't lean toward a particular belief system (as I don't), the Relationship and the Path will still function exactly the same for you if you engage with the guidelines outlined in this book.

Not so fast, you may be thinking. *It worked for your coworker even though she* wasn't *following the guidelines in this book.* Indeed. That's because the rules of how the Universe works are the same regardless of whether we are conscious of them or not—just like gravity. Hooray for that! There's nothing more disheartening than feeling like we are living in chaos where nothing makes sense. Whether you are actively walking your Spiritual Path or not, the experience is consistent.

The benefit of consciously engaging with the process is that you won't need someone to nudge you in the right direction most of the time because you yourself will understand how the Universe works. You will be able to leap over hurdles using your own guidance system. Magical moments will no longer happen accidentally or feel once-in-a-lifetime; instead, they become the fabric of your daily life. You will understand why impediments appear on your Path and can apply your energy to removing them or finding an alternate solution.

Did it feel good to help my co-worker? Sure. We all need outside help sometimes, myself included. But I'm happiest when people can consciously navigate their own challenges. My favorite stories are those that people share of facing their own tough Soulwork and finding the means to clear their Path. We can *always* offer each other support and encouragement, though, as we all work through our own soul challenges.

THE COST OF NOT DOING OUR SOULWORK

Our Soulwork influences us whether we like it or not. When we ignore it, we get stuck in situations that inhibit our ability to learn and grow. We repeat patterns absent of understanding their cause. Without our Relationship with the Universe to bolster us up or the Spiritual Path to infuse our work with meaning, over time, this struggle can lead to depression,[1] restlessness, ennui, and existential crisis.

We might end a relationship with a controlling partner, for example, only to find ourselves, unexpectedly, in *another* relationship with a controlling partner. *How could this happen when they seemed so different in the beginning?* Often, we think the people, environment, or circumstances in our lives need to change—when it is *we* who need to change.

If we don't resolve the underlying Soulwork triggering the pattern to surface, we will continue to find ourselves in the same types of situations. The Universe is trying to help us *see* the problem. Once we see it, the effect on our lives becomes apparent, and we can finally work on fixing the *source* of the issue. If we're oblivious, we can't fix anything; we simply suffer through.

---

[1]   This book contains advice and information relating to overall health and well-being. It should be used to supplement rather than replace the advice of your doctor or another trained health professional. If you know or suspect you have a health problem, it is recommended that you seek your physician's advice before embarking on any medical program or treatment. The publisher and author disclaim liability for any medical outcome that may occur as a result of applying the methods described in this book.

This may seem unfair, but it parallels how we teach our own children and students in life. We give them lots of opportunities to attempt a skill until they've mastered it. If they fail in a critical area, we make them repeatedly practice, in different ways, until they've got it. The same is true for our souls. Until we've learned whatever we are meant to learn, we cannot move beyond the pattern.

Unfortunately, there is plenty of distraction in the world to keep us in ignorance. If we don't have our Spiritual Path or Relationship with the Universe to support us on our journey, it can feel like the world is "against us" or that life is an uphill climb. We'll find many others with good intentions willing to empathize. We all need compassion—especially self-compassion—and we need space to heal our own wounds free from judgment. But sometimes, we over-emphasize the symptoms of our struggles because we have no idea what the roots of our problems are. If we're not doing our Soulwork, we're not finding and resolving those underlying conditions, which means the Universe will just *keep poking them*.

Although we cannot make others appreciate us or force the world to see us as we wish to be seen, we *can* work on how our soul scars and core challenges get in the way of our own happiness, success, and love. We can develop the skills to engage with our lives so that we learn at an accelerated pace. And, we can blow through barriers to achieve our highest potential.

2

RULES OF THE "ROAD"

Defining Soulwork, the Spiritual Path, and the
Relationship with the Universe

Before we leap off a cliff in enthusiasm to begin, we need to cover a few things. Any good guide will lay out the ground rules before an expedition to provide context for the journey and help keep us safe. It's the same here.

I'd like to start by delving a little deeper into a few of the terms I've been throwing around to clarify their meaning and explain how they relate to each other.

Our **Soulwork,** for example, is the work of finding, navigating, and addressing the wounds and fears that inhibit our spiritual evolution, but also developing the gifts through which we contribute to the human experience. Soulwork differs from adversity. Where adversity is encountered through the external circumstances we're challenged to face, Soulwork represents our interior conditions. Adversity may *lead* us to Soulwork, but accomplishing our Soulwork always requires an *internal shift*.

What if we get laid off from our job? (A perceived adverse event in most people's lives.) As we start searching for a new position, we may discover a fear of rejection that hampers us from applying for roles that would *advance* our career rather than keep us operating at the same comfortable level. Examining and resolving that underlying fear is part of our Soulwork.

When we become aware of Soulwork, our mission is to engage with it—healing our wounds, dealing with our blocking beliefs, and finding our gifts. It would be nice to solely concentrate on cultivating and using our talents. But for most of us—myself included—they are shrouded beneath layers of coping mechanisms that hide deep-seated worries about rejection and self-worth. Contending with our internal constraints clears the way for us to discover and express our genius.

The **Spiritual Path** is the winding road of soul evolution, the structured process of growth and development that reveals the central work of our soul. The more actively we engage with our Path, the more quickly we find and fulfill our Soulwork. Our path is not paved in stone. In fact, sometimes, we'll feel like we must machete our way through the underbrush to make progress. When we're mired in a murky fog, though, we can lean on our Relationship with the Universe and our Guides to help light the way.

Our **Relationship with the Universe** is our connection to the energy within and without. All the Universe is made up of energy, as are we. The Universe guides us through signs and messages we receive in the *external* world. When I started applying the guidance in those messages to help me navigate my Soulwork, I noticed a type of "response"—a path would unblock, a wish would be granted, something seemingly magical would happen, or maybe I would just *feel* amazing. (Don't underestimate the power of that last one; plenty of people become addicted to alternative substances solely for that feeling of bliss.) Over time, a pattern emerged, a type of dialogue that played out across my life.

For the first decade and a half of my journey, I only thought of myself as having a Relationship with the Universe. I considered the signs I witnessed as coming from the "Universe." Between 2012 and 2015, I started to explore the concept of having Spirit Guides or Guardian Angels specific to me. I owe all credit for that avenue of exploration to the teachings of Sonia Choquette.

Where our Relationship to the Universe is general, our **Guides** are specific to us. The exchanges we have with them can be very personal—like we have unseen friends around when we need them. Music is one way my Guides interact with me, and they've delivered several messages through surprising tracks that play over my car's Bluetooth connection or on my phone. After one recent disastrous date, when I turned the car's ignition, my Guides blasted the Queen song "Another One Bites the Dust" through the speakers. I had to laugh.

Making sense of the difference between our Relationship with the Universe and our relationship with our Guides can be tricky. A mental model that I find helpful is types of light. The energy of the Universe is like the luminosity of the sun. During the day, the sun shines its radiance across the surface of the side of our planet that faces it (let's ignore clouds, shade, caves, and such for the moment). If I go outside, sunlight shines down on me. If you go outside, it shines on you. The light and heat I receive from the sun don't take away from the light and heat you receive from the sun. The sun's energy is available to us all. Similarly, the energy of the Universe is around us all the time—it is the energy of all things living and non—and equally available to us all. We interact with this energy automatically, but we can improve our lives by engaging in the Relationship more consciously.

Where the energy of the Universe is like the illumination of the sun, our Guides are like the lights in our homes. Both the sun and our home fixtures are light sources in our lives. We all share the sunlight, but our lanterns and lamps are unique to us. Our neighbors may have different lights. Similarly, we all connect to the energy of the Universe but have

Spirit Guides or Guardian Angels specific to us. We tend to use our home lights most when the sun's glow isn't strong enough to help us see clearly. The relationship with our Guides can work this way as well—we might need them most when the Path seems dark, when the way forward is uncertain, and we're trying to find our way back to the light of the sun (or at least hold out till it rises again).

If the term *Guides* feels awkward to you, you might think of receiving this unseen assistance from Angels or your great aunt Susie who passed on a few years ago. Find a way of thinking about your Relationship with the Universe and secret support system that resonates for you and use that. When we feel comfortable, we open up, and when we open up to the possibilities of invisible aid, our lives really take flight.

THE RULES OF ENGAGEMENT

Now that we have defined the most critical terms, let's cover some essential ground rules I have observed repeatedly on my own journey and in witnessing the journeys of others. I share them now, hoping they provide some background as you walk your own Path. Awareness of these helps reduce frustration and confusion about how the Universe works. Some ideas may make sense right away; others may reveal their value further along. Keep them in mind as you traverse the nebulous terrain of the Spiritual Path.

1. THE UNIVERSE WILL NEVER ASK YOU TO HARM YOURSELF OR ANOTHER HUMAN BEING.

The Universe does not need any help hurting people. Causing pain and suffering is simple. Bringing joy and love into the world is the far harder task. If this seems obvious, great! One of the most serious risks of walking the Spiritual Path and developing a Relationship with the Universe *is* delusion. This point cannot be over-emphasized. Many people who have committed horrific violence in this world have done so based on a false belief their actions were "guided" by a higher power. We think of people who perpetrate such insidious acts as evil, but sometimes they do so in the name of their faith, or because of their love and devotion to a specific cause.

Connection to the Universe can be euphoric, triggering altered conscious states equivalent to intoxication or a chemical high. We know that people under such influences can sometimes make bad decisions or draw delusional conclusions. I highlight this risk as Rule #1 because it is imperative we don't underestimate it.

If you feel guided to do anything deliberately harmful to yourself or someone else, take a step back, examine your motives more mindfully, and seek professional help.

2. THE RELATIONSHIP WITH THE UNIVERSE FUNCTIONS ALMOST EXACTLY LIKE A PHYSICAL RELATIONSHIP.

In many ways, our Relationship with the Universe operates the same as any human relationship we have.

- The more seriously we take the Relationship and the more we respect it, the more meaningful it will be.
- The more we engage with guidance we receive, the more responsive and relevant our interactions will be.

Granting our Relationship gravitas in our lives doesn't mean we have to adopt all the advice that comes through. Although our Guides have an expanded awareness of the energy in motion around us, they are not omniscient and the future isn't set in stone. Thus, even our Guides can only provide insight based on what is currently knowable.

However, our Guides *do* know what Soulwork we confront, and they want to help us with that. Why do they support our spiritual development? Because we are *all* part of the energy of the Universe. Helping our energy field heal and grow affects the whole Universe, the way a few drops of food coloring can tint a full glass. When we learn, our Guides also learn, and the entire Universe grows in understanding.

Can your partner do your job for you? Can your father write your book for you? Can your child make your marriage work? For the most part, no.

The Universe and our Guides cannot *do* our work for us—they can point us in the right direction, aid in clearing the path forward, or help us get out of our own way. Our Guides can facilitate meaningful connections with others, put opportunities in front of us, and support and encourage us in engaging with our Soulwork. Having other expectations of what a Relationship with the Universe can "do" for us might reflect a secret desire to get out of the Soulwork we're meant to address. I have certainly been guilty of such wishful thinking. There is plenty of magic in the relationship as is—you will see this for yourself.

How is the Relationship with the Universe different from a physical relationship?

Unlike many physical relationships, our Relationship with the Universe will always be with us. We never lose it. *We* may turn away from our connection in shame or frustration, but our Guides and the Universe are always ready to be re-engaged, thrilled to support us on our journey if we're willing to do our work, eager to light the way to the next level of self-realization and co-creation.

An obvious difference between our physical life relationships and our Relationship with the Universe is that we can see and perceive the people who make up our human relationships. In our Relationship with the Universe? Not so much. Hence, some of the earliest milestones on the Path reflect taking the Relationship seriously enough to work with advice from a non-empirical source.

3. OUR SOULWORK LEADS US TOWARD ALIGNMENT.

We are aligned when every aspect of our being—our mind, body, heart, and soul—orients towards the same purpose or goal. Co-creation, what we think of as "magically getting what we want" or things just "falling into place," happens automatically when we are aligned. You don't need to know the guidelines I'm laying out for co-creation to occur. But often, we are not aligned. Understanding these fundamental rules helps us diagnose the problem when co-creation *isn't* happening.

In attempting to align the aspects of ourselves, we'll find our pieces all have different personalities. The body is like that friend who will go along with almost anything—it's onboard, as long as we're taking care of it. If we're not, our own lack of self-care may inhibit our ability to co-create. The heart and soul are *usually* aligned, but when they're not—things can get *really* tough. The most frequent challenge, though, is bringing the mind into alignment with the rest of our being. Easily influenced by external factors, other people, and familial or cultural conditioning, the mind can be noisy about what it wants. The mind intends to bring the rest of us into alignment with the external world because that makes it easier to maneuver in society. This reflects what the mind has been taught: how it's been trained.

To the periodic frustration of the rest of our being, especially our minds, our life objectives are set at the soul level. This is our Soulwork. To the frequent frustration of our soul, the other aspects of our being (our body, heart, and mind) *also* require regular attention and care. In dire situations, their needs can trump even the soul's goals. All our aspects realize, with more or less enthusiasm—sometimes *comically* less enthusiasm—that they need to play nicely with each other if we're ever going to accomplish anything in life.

One of our ultimate challenges (and achievements!) in walking the Spiritual Path, then, is to recognize when all our aspects are *not* getting along—because it means we're out of alignment.

Several years ago, I discussed co-creation, which had been integral to my life for twenty years at that point, with my then-husband.[2]

"Well, if you could do that," he commented, "why don't you co-create a million dollars?"

To which I promptly replied, "Because I don't want a million dollars."

"That's ridiculous," he shot back. "Everyone wants a million dollars."

But is that really true? Let me ask you this. If someone *gave* you a million dollars, but you could never spend a single cent, would you want it?

Probably not. The million dollars is a 'stand-in' for what you *really* want. The Universe doesn't recognize stand-ins, though, as we saw with my co-worker who was trying to manifest her move by focusing on getting a job. Although *mentally,* many people would *like* to have a million dollars, their hearts and souls really wish for *other* things that their *minds* think a million dollars will help them get (or at least allow them to pursue). But since the money itself isn't a soul-level wish, it cannot be co-created.[3] And, focusing the mind on money while the heart and soul have different aims sends mixed signals to the Universe, inhibiting co-creation.

Once we align to what we *really* want at a soul level, solutions to achieve those goals and desires magically appear. We cannot force ourselves into alignment. But, happily, alignment is our *natural* state. If we're *not*

---

[2]   I feel compelled to note that this conversation happened a couple years *before* the one where he said "Beth doesn't look for jobs, jobs look for Beth."

[3]   It would be incorrect to say that everyone who has won a million dollars in life has come to that money through co-creation. However, it is impossible to *co-create* a million dollars for ourselves if we are *not* in alignment. (In other words, you might win a million dollars by chance, but you *cannot* co-create it.) The concept of "chance" is real. Chance events happen because the future *isn't* set in stone. If the Universe did not allow unexpected change, we couldn't make our own decisions and grow. The same instability, or openness, in the energetic system that permits change/growth (or free will) creates the conditions for chance events to occur.

aligned, a piece of Soulwork we need to address is almost always standing in the way. Fortunately, the more we engage with our Soulwork, the more quickly we can spot areas of misalignment and attend to resolving them.

4. WHEN WE ARE MISALIGNED TOO LONG, THE UNIVERSE STEPS IN.

This rule causes the most heartache in our lives. When we allow ourselves to persist in a misaligned state, the Universe will "help" us realign. The Universe will respond to an SOS call from our heart, body, or soul—even if we don't consciously know we are sending one. Such SOS calls can lead to events like job loss, relationship breakups, failure of projects we're working on, and sometimes even bodily injury or disease. This doesn't mean that every adverse event in our lives represents an SOS call from our inner being. Even when an event has a rational and explainable cause, though, there may *also* be a soul-level cause.

Sometimes we find ourselves dealing with the results of an SOS call from someone else's soul, which might manifest as a job ending because the business owner decides they need to spend more time with their family. It might manifest as a relationship ending because our partner needs to follow their heart in a different direction. Or perhaps a parent, child, or sibling reveals an intensely personal secret that has held them hostage, but the revelation also impacts our lives.

Even considering these examples, many events in our lives happen in response to *our own* misalignment. At the very least, it's a perspective worth exploring when we feel negatively impacted by a change.

Our heart, soul, and body can signal their distress, but, unfortunately, we don't get to decide the means of rescue. *I wanted something different,* we think, *but I didn't want this.* Over time, as we develop confidence handling our Soulwork, we learn to *feel* when we are out of alignment. This presents us with the opportunity to take our own steps toward re-alignment, allowing the Universe to assist our conscious efforts rather than devising its own solution.

At the tail end of 2019, I felt stuck in my job. I loved my boss, my co-workers, and the company I worked for, but, over the years, I had grown out of alignment with the position; I was stagnating. I supported four different teams simultaneously, but I felt most fulfilled in my work with one team. In my heart, I wished I could work in that group, but none of them worked in Chicago; it seemed like an impossible move. The misalignment caused by my staying in the position increasingly tightened around my chest, unseen hands pulling strings on a corset. Something needed to change, and I knew it. So I resolved to start looking for a position outside the company.

Imagine my surprise, then, in early March of 2020, when our central team dispersed into the groups we supported. Suddenly, I joined the very team I had hoped for! I had recognized that the situation wasn't working, that I needed to address my own realignment—and the Universe stepped in to grant my wish.

The only remaining challenge was that I still assisted four different teams, only reporting to one of them. To complicate matters, the responsibilities associated with my role had increased significantly, and I was stretched way too thin. I worried that I would disappoint my new group because of my crushing responsibilities to other groups. After a couple of months of suffering under this weight, I planned to talk to my boss about the situation, but I wasn't sure what he could do. I wished that I could just support my primary team.

A couple months later, my group moved into a completely different line of business. The other three portfolios on my desk stayed behind; all that weight just *disappeared,* like magic.

Now that I can focus solely on that team, I'm happier in my job than I have been in years. Such are the benefits of avoiding limiting beliefs and attending to our own alignment.

5. THE UNIVERSE PROVIDES SOLUTIONS FOR THE HIGHEST GOALS OF OUR SOUL, NOT "COP-OUTS."

Remember in Rule #3, when I brought up my heart not wanting a million dollars? Well, after my husband of seventeen years exited our marriage, I really, *really* wanted to win that million dollars. First, it would have solved the financial challenges brought on by the divorce. It would have allowed me to follow my passion in writing about and working with people on their Spiritual Paths. But mostly, it would have been a great way to *stick it to him* after we were no longer together. *You didn't think I could co-create a million dollars? There! See! I did it!*

I started to think I could, too. People win the lottery. It happens. I have an excellent Relationship with the Universe—why shouldn't I be able to get a few measly numbers right?

Except…a small voice protested (annoyingly, I might add), winning a million dollars might solve a few problems, but it wouldn't bring me any closer to my *soul's* goals. A few months before my marriage collapsed, I discovered some Soulwork around inferiority that sometimes surfaced as small and stealthy jealousy of my then-husband's success. *Don't you want to rise through your own efforts?* My heart whispered. *You can do it. If you win the lottery, your ability to support yourself financially will be forever tied to that. How can you heal your feeling of inferiority if a chance event resolves all your problems?*

And then, of course, I'm back to Rule #3; I *know* I can't co-create a lottery win because my heart and soul don't support that wish. Instead, a number of ideas bubbled up (one of them being this book) that might help me resolve some of my financial challenges. As my Guides gently turned me away from a path that didn't match my soul's goals, they illuminated several other paths that might.

The Universe will not assist us in bypassing our Soulwork. If we feel blocked on a path, usually it means a piece of Soulwork is sitting in front of us that we don't want to see.

6. THE UNIVERSE DOES NOT ACTUALLY CARE WHAT WE DO. *(with some footnotes, obviously)*

This one may seem confusing until we unpack it. When we imagine our life purpose, we might feel drawn to specific career callings. For example, we may think it is our life purpose to make music, teach, create art, or invent the next technology breakthrough because we believe these to be more "noble" pursuits than whatever we're doing with our lives at the time.

However, beware the trap of believing that the work we *want* to do is the work we were *meant* to do. We can spend years of our life trying to get to a particular outcome or career path, only to discover that it isn't what we thought. When we operate from a conviction that some work is *better* than other work, we can unconsciously excuse ourselves from the Soulwork tied to where we are right now.

In her online Six Sensory training course, Sonia Choquette tells of watching a holy man tend a hotel shrine in India. "Every day, he would light the candles, he would sing, he would place the flower petals, he would smile at us," she said. "He was so happy just being there and doing that every day." We can get caught up in dreams of grandeur when our lives, just as they are, could be the temples we tend with joy and love.

In many cultures, including the Western Judeo-Christian tradition, we have been trained to deny the self in favor of service to others, which can lead to a belief that converting others, convincing others, or even aiding others is our life's purpose. Helping others is always admirable, but *sometimes* it can be a subconscious excuse to get out of our own Soulwork. When the primary focus of our lives is around the health, happiness, and well-being of others, it can shift our focus off the self and the Soulwork *we* are meant to do.

The Universe and our Guides help us achieve *our* soul's objectives. A life in service can be a beautiful thing; we just need to ensure that we do it because *we* want to—that the sacrifices we make to live such a life are our *choice*. Not because it's a moral imperative, a salve to our guilt, a "noble" pursuit, or somehow makes us feel better than others. Such reasons may reflect our need to carve out an identity for ourselves, more than they are about actual service.

Actual service overflows from the heart with no strings attached. If we're not feeling that, we don't need to stop helping; we just *also* need to prioritize taking care of ourselves and the work of our own soul.

Now, honestly, who knows the mind of God? I certainly don't. So maybe you really are doing God's work. What I do know, without a doubt, though, is that the most dangerous risk of spiritual work, regardless of the method through which it's approached, is delusion. The chief value of keeping Rule #6 in our back pocket is that it keeps us firmly planted on the safe side of sanity. We are safest when we remember that we don't live our lives on behalf of anyone else—seen or unseen, human or divine. We own our own journey and our own choices.

The Universe does not care if you're a mailperson, a banker, a teacher, a priest, a doctor, a salesperson, or an actress. We may engage in behaviors in our chosen vocation that create additional Soulwork we must address, but the Universe is mostly indifferent to *what* we choose to do with our lives.

Imagine the Universe as a giant benevolent parent. As parents, do we care if our toddler is playing with blocks, coloring, cooking in the kiddie kitchen, or playing dress-up? Probably not. However, if we notice that our child always demands her own way, never asserts himself, manifests anger through physical violence, or demonstrates self-loathing—these are things we care about. Such behaviors will trip our children up *whatever* they are doing in life, and they need to be addressed.

And so it is with each of us.

The Universe will put situations on our Paths to help us see and work on our Soulwork. What we do with the rest of our lives is up to us.

3

THE DOUBLE AGENT OF CHANGE

Introducing an Essential Guide on Our Spiritual Path

While working on a blog post about psychedelics and the transcendent experience in the spring of 2015, I recalled a quote from Lewis Hyde's book *Trickster Makes this World* that would be perfect to launch the piece. Grabbing my e-reader, I entered the words I remembered from the quote into the search function. No results. I tried a few different combinations but fared no better. Then I noticed a small, printed phrase at the bottom of my search window that read, "This book has not been indexed."

Not been indexed? I was going to have to dig through the book manually? Argh! How badly did I want this quote?

An e-reader is not really designed for skimming, but I tried that first anyway. Skipping around based on the table of contents, I glanced through pages here and there, but that didn't get me anywhere. I would have to slow-read the book from page one. *Fine.*

With a warrior frame of mind—this book was not going to best *me*—I started from the beginning. As the words wound their way through my consciousness, though, something curious began to unfold in my brain. I had planned to write a piece about Trickster and the Spiritual Path since the beginning of my blog over a year prior, but I hadn't gotten around to it and, frankly, wasn't planning to work on it for quite a few months more.

But in re-reading Lewis Hyde's work, I suddenly realized Trickster was *the* most valuable topic I could be writing about. All other work either faded into the background or became somehow dependent on my laying out the concept of Trickster. With my mind racing through how to structure the post, I began to laugh, for right there was Trickster's influence in action. I knew in that moment a Trickster post was the very next thing I was going to write. I would never have chosen this course of action if I hadn't been "forced" to re-start the book. And, of course, the beauty of the trick was that even though I was on to it, I *wanted* to write this post—nothing excited me more. The trap had been perfectly set. I was snared.

I thought my Trickster fixation would end with the completion of that long-ago blog entry. I was so, so wrong. Suddenly, I began seeing Trickster's influence everywhere—from the lyrics of the musical *Hamilton* to within the pages of Michael Pollan's book *Cooked*. Everything I was interested in somehow seemed to trace back to Trickster. He was in my life to stay.

Who is Trickster, and why do we care?

That's a more challenging question to answer than you could ever imagine, but I'll take a crack at it anyway.

In North America, Trickster is known by many monikers: Coyote, Raven, Inktomi the Spider-Man, Rabbit, and Wakdjunkaga, just to name a few. The Greeks knew him as Hermes and the Romans as Mercury. In Africa, he is Anansi or, sometimes, Legba. Pacific Islanders usually call him Maui. In the ancient Vedic texts, Trickster is Krishna, and to the Vikings, he is Loki. If thinking of Trickster in polytheistic terms is uncomfortable, note that even the well-known religions of today usually have some sort of Trickster figure. The Muslims find Trickster in stories of the Mullah Nasrudin. And in Buddhist tales, Trickster might show up as a monkey or fox. There are Trickster aspects of Jesus, too, a concept I have found fascinating to explore.[4]

In some cultures, Trickster helps birth the world into being. In others, he ushers in its end.

Trickster is the original disruptor—the embodiment of curiosity and craftiness. Both inventor and thief, Trickster sometimes steals ideas and often steals actual things. Never bothered by the dictates of polite society, he frequently flouts rules of all kind. Often, he gets away with crossing a boundary, breaking new ground, and opening the world up to a new idea. Other times, he does not—suffering embarrassment, ostracization, or physical harm for daring to ignore a line. As human beings living in an age of innovation and disruption, we can all relate to that. Trickster thrives through his charm and wit, and his ability to shine the light of humor into the darkest moments makes him a transformative figure in whatever mythos we find him.

IS TRICKSTER REAL?

All of this is interesting, but Trickster is an ancient *mythological* figure, not a *real-life* figure—so how does this relate to our practical experience

---

[4]   I recognize that Judaism is missing from this list. My apologies for that. Unfortunately, Judaism is the major world religion I am least familiar with. It felt inauthentic to speak about it as if I have more knowledge than I do. I was raised Catholic, married a Presbyterian-turned-atheist, and have studied mystical and alternative elements in Christianity. I studied Hinduism, Buddhism, and Islam in college, so I already had that background when I encountered Trickster. But my knowledge of Judaism is, sadly, inadequate, not to mention Judaism and Trickster. Of course, the upside is that it leaves the door open for someone else to write about Judaism and Trickster elements, which I would certainly find a fascinating topic.

of walking the Spiritual Path, our Relationship with the Universe, and doing our Soulwork?

Is Trickster real?

We who write about, study, and work with this character all dance around the subject. It sounds ridiculous to say he's real—and yet, I experience Trickster as a real influence in my life and work, a feeling that seems shared by fellow devotees. In their compilation of Trickster essays, *Mythical Trickster Figures: Contours, Contexts, and Criticisms*, editors William J. Hynes and William G. Doty write, "One might say that [Trickster's] presence is felt in the writing of this book…constantly disassembling and deconstructing it."[5]

Karl Kerenyi, lauded as one of the founders of modern interpretation of Greek mythology, experienced his relationship with Trickster on a personal level. In an excerpt from his diary on April 1, 1952,[6] he inquires, "Does Hermes wish to play the same game with me again?"

Kerenyi's wife, Magda, references her husband's relationship with Trickster in the prefatory note to his work *Hermes, Guide of Souls*. She states, "finding and losing belong to the ambivalent sphere of the 'god of journey,' who so often put into Kerenyi's hand just the right reading material for a voyage."[7] She goes on to say that the word *Hermaion,* meaning a gift of Hermes meant for her husband that "a book or an article unexpectedly appeared at hand in the right moment, even independently of traveling.[8]

On my Spiritual Path, I see Trickster's hand in every fortuitous find and every symbolic loss. I hear his chuckle when I land in a mess of my own making and his cheer when I evade a trap.

---

[5] William J. Hynes & William G. Doty, *Mythical Trickster Figures: Contours, Contexts, and Criticisms* (University Alabama Press; Revised ed. Edition, June 15, 2009), Amazon Digital Services, Loc 795 out of 5355, Kindle.

[6] What a delicious coincidence that he wrote this on April *Fool's* Day!

[7] Karl Kerenyi, *Hermes, Guide of Souls* (New York: Spring Publications, Inc., 2008), 6

[8] Ibid

But what, then, is Trickster? Is he a god? An energetic being? A mental model? Or simply an aid to our imagination?

We each benefit from developing our own relationship with Trickster on our Spiritual Path. If thinking of him as a defined entity is uncomfortable, you can use the idea of "Trickster energy" instead—focusing on how this energy shows up in your life rather than worrying about "who" causes it. Avoiding Trickster energy out of fear or discomfort limits our learning potential, though, so I encourage you to find a way to work with it. Embrace the opportunity to look at yourself and the world through the lenses that Trickster provides in whatever way feels right for you.

THE ROAD-BUT-NOT-ROAD

In his book, *Trickster Makes This World*, Lewis Hyde tells us, "The road Trickster travels is a spirit road as well as a road in fact. He is the adept who can move between heaven and earth and between the living and the dead."[9]

This is not to say that Trickster is formally recognized as the god of the road in every culture where he appears, but, in most mythologies, he can usually be found *on* it. Many Native American Trickster stories start with Trickster wandering around on a road or in the spaces between settlements. Greek stories of Hermes and Norse stories of Loki frequently find them, too, on the road.

Roads seem simple, yet they have a strangely dual role, acting as both connecting and dividing lines. Roads join cities and divide neighborhoods. I had a friend in high school whose road was buried in snow every winter as her block straddled the dividing line between two villages. Neither wanted to own plowing the street.

---

[9]   Lewis Hyde, *Trickster Makes this World* (Farrar, Straus, and Giroux; Illustrated edition, August 17 2010), 6

The road leads us from home to see the world, and on the road, we return. We think of a road as a place of impermanence—one travels a road; one does not live on a road. Even for those who *do* live on the road, it's hardly considered a fixed existence, situated in one spot. But at the Chicago History Museum some years ago, I saw an exhibit showcasing historical maps of the city from the days of first settlement to the present. Some of the oldest versions featured Native American trails that, when overlaid with modern maps, still operate as main streets today. Roads are usually a symbol of transience—and yet, across the world, sometimes they outlast the very civilizations that trod the grass into dust to create them.

The Spiritual Path endures the same way. No matter what mythology, religion, or language overlays it, the underlying structure of the Path is the same. And whatever road we're on, spiritual, or physical, or both, we're going to bump into Trickster.

Most people have never heard of Trickster. When they *do* know of him, it's usually in his most disruptive roles, playing tricks and laying traps. There is far more to Trickster than this, but even the shifty aspect of his character is instructive. On our Spiritual Path, Trickster both trips us up *and* helps us out. Understanding how he operates trains us to find our opportunities for greatest transformation while avoiding the traps of self-deception and delusion. Hyde tells us:

> "In the Okanagan creation story, the Great Spirit, having told Coyote that he must show the New People how to catch salmon, goes on to say, 'I have important work for you to do. There are many bad creatures on earth. You will have to kill them, otherwise they will eat the New People.' The myth says, then, that there are large devouring forces in this world, and that Trickster's intelligence arose not just to feed himself, but to outwit these other eaters."[10]

---

[10] Ibid, 22

When we think of "people-devouring beasts" from a spiritual perspective, what else could these be but our own subconscious fears and wounds that eat away at us from the inside? On the Spiritual Path, we must face these dark and disconcerting parts of ourselves to find peace and renew our spirit. This is part of our Soulwork.

"Trickster commonly relies on his prey to help him spring the traps he makes." [11] If it is Trickster's job to kill the devouring beasts that would eat us from the inside, then he must lay the kind of trap that ensures we *see* them. "The fleetness of large herbivores is part of their natural defense against predators." Hyde tells us, "Coyote...takes advantage of that instinctual defense by directing the beasts into the sun and toward a cliff, so that fleetness itself backfires."[12]

When we walk the Spiritual Path, our central identity comes under intense scrutiny. Qualities we think of as strengths can, in some situations, be the weaknesses that bring us down. The traits we judge in others may be rooted in our own subconscious fears and prejudices. When we're enmeshed in a difficult situation, sometimes it's a mess of our own making. If we dig a bit further down, we usually find an unacknowledged piece of Soulwork that triggered our behavior. It is part of Trickster's job to reveal our Soulwork, and tripping us up may be the only way to force us to *see* the problem.

We should take heart, though, that "Coyote can imagine the fish trap precisely because he's been a fish himself."[13] Only by having been both caught in traps and a designer of traps has Trickster become an authoritative guide and teacher. With all his trap-springing and beast-killing, Trickster is, really, teaching us to be like him—to learn from our mistakes, to adapt to changing circumstances, to recognize that not only can our strengths be our greatest weaknesses, but what we thought of as weaknesses can become our greatest strengths. At its core, this message

---

[11]   Ibid, 19
[12]   Ibid, 17
[13]   Ibid, 20

is hopeful. We may be caught in a trap today, but—if we learn—perhaps we can dance around the next one.

Although Trickster is associated with a wide range of aspects of life, he has governance over four primary areas: lenses through which we can view our Path and the world. Trickster acts as guardian of the boundary, governor of binding and releasing, administrator of what is lost and found, and authority over what is hidden and revealed.

Sometimes we trick ourselves into believing that the way we see life is the only one there is—or, at least, the only *right* one. Using the lenses of Trickster to view ourselves, our Path, and our environment reminds us that even our own perception is just another *lens*, interchangeable with many others. The more lenses through which we can look at the world, the more we learn.

DRAWING THE LINE

In his oldest and most fundamental role, Trickster is guardian of the *boundary*. Hermes, Trickster of the ancient Greeks, is believed to take his name from the stone pillars and cairns, called *herms*, that marked the boundaries of tribal territory. Similarly, a world away in Africa, the boundary guardian Legba might have a stone pillar shrine at a village gate. This role is so closely tied to Trickster's primary essence that all his other traits, including his role as Spiritual Path guide, flow and evolve from it.

Boundaries define our experience. They can be geographic, technological, legal, cultural, moral, sexual, mental, and deeply, deeply personal. Boundaries determine what we will and won't do, what we do and don't say, where we will and won't go, and even what we do and don't believe.

Boundaries are meant to be challenged, tested, and sometimes overcome—but without any, we would have chaos.

When we think of the Chinese symbol for universal balance—the yin yang—we notice the juxtaposition of darkness and light, each with a little bit of the other contained within. We notice the apparent motion of the two opposing forces, but we rarely notice the lines that keep all these various components apart. There is no balance—there is no symbol—without the boundaries that separate yin from yang. Erase them, and we have only an amorphous gray blob.

The Spiritual Path asks us to examine our own boundaries. What do we believe is possible? What are we afraid to do? Where do we limit ourselves? How do we define who we are? All of these are boundary questions we meet along the Path. Trickster can guide us on whether a boundary needs to be crossed to help us grow or if we should hold the line. Through awareness of and experimentation with our own borders, we discover who we really are and the path to who we want to be.

We can use this lens on the Path to explore the areas in life where we are rigid or when we become uncomfortable—the boundaries of our comfort zone.

Several years ago, I struggled with the concept of intuition. Even with a decade of experience navigating external guidance from the Universe, when it came to my "gut feelings," I couldn't easily separate my inner voice from my wishful thinking or fears.

At the time, I treated Sonia Choquette's book *22 Life Lessons* as a spiritual development workbook. I would randomly flip to a page and work on the lesson it represented for about a month (or longer, if needed). The second time I consulted the book for advice, a voice in my head clearly directed, "Turn to page 32." When I did, I found a chapter titled "Follow Your Inner Voice." What a coincidence.

I grappled with this lesson for a few months without making any headway. Then, at some point, it occurred to me that Tarot might be a way to bridge the gap, to ease my way into consulting my intuition without relying on the "voices" in my head.

My Catholic upbringing imbued me with considerable resistance to Tarot, though, and goosebumps prickled my arms at the thought of violating this unspoken family taboo. Yet, what did I really know about Tarot?

Nothing.

I decided to check out a couple of books on the subject. It was just reading. How hazardous could that be?

At the time, I did not think I would ever own a deck, but reading about Tarot helped relieve much of my anxiety. After all, on some level, it's just a deck of cards. Fantastical histories aside, the most reliable origination story of the Tarot marks its creation in Italy during the Renaissance period as a card game. Tarot's function as a divination tool only came later. Historically, things as innocuous as tea leaves, sticks, and coins have been used for similar divination practices. But while people still use tea leaves and coins for practical purposes, with Tarot, the original form of entertainment fell away. Only its use in divination has persisted (although you can still find the rules for the game on the internet, and derivative trump-related card games are still prevalent in many cultures).[14]

In a way, using a Tarot deck was just another medium for work I was already doing. It's the energy we bring to the cards that determines their use. I could always get a deck and see how it felt to use it for guidance, I reasoned. If I suffered any distress, I could just get rid of them.

More than one book mentioned that, traditionally, a Tarot deck had to be gifted. The chances of that happening within my then-circle of family, friends, and acquaintances weren't just zero; they were absolute zero. This didn't bother me, though. Having made my decision, I was excited about

---

[14] https://en.wikipedia.org/wiki/Tarot_card_games

finding my own deck. I knew it would be a "gift" from the Universe, a *Hermaion* (although I had not yet met Trickster), and it was.

My very first reading was only three cards, yet it shined the way through a Dark Night of the Soul I had been enmeshed in for *years*. On another occasion, I consulted my deck after the birth of my youngest daughter when her four-month appointment revealed some disturbing news. She had lost so much weight, she'd fallen from the 20th to the 3rd percentile (meaning 97% of babies weighed more than she did at that age). She had been consuming all my pumped milk and constantly feeding when I was home. I was worried beyond measure and baffled how to solve the problem.

When I consulted the deck, the Ace of Cups came up. This card symbolically means a new emotional beginning. Yet it was the imagery that captured my attention. A single chalice with water sloshing over the rim. Could milk be spilling out of the bottles somehow?

Usually, our nanny fed our daughter when I was at the office, and I breastfed her at home, but the next day I asked the nanny to give her a bottle in the morning while I observed from all angles. I noticed tiny but steady dripping from the cap on the underside of the bottle—they were literally leaking.

"I just thought she was spitting up a lot," the nanny said.

Upon investigation, not all the bottle caps leaked, just some. And after we disposed of all the faulty caps, my daughter started gaining weight again. Who knows when we would have figured it out if I hadn't consulted my deck, not to mention been too scared to ever use one in the first place.

Exploring our edges can be unnerving, but crossing a boundary often starts with a single step. We don't have to high-dive into the deep; we can wade into the shallow end of our unease. But we can't expand and grow if we forever stay within our self-constructed walls.

Exercise: *Often, our boundaries are most visible in what we're afraid of. Think of several topics, activities, or people that inspire fear or discomfort. Journal about what triggers those emotions within you and see if you can detect what boundaries they bump up against.*

Pick one of these, whichever you feel most drawn to (or the most averse to, if you're feeling ambitious), and spend about a month exploring this area of discomfort. Exploration can take the form of research, meditation, or journaling. If you choose to focus on a person who triggers aversion or irritation, try devoting time to sending them positive energy or engaging with them in a more conscious, active way. If it's an activity, find a way to engage with that activity, even if only through research or as a spectator.*

If you haven't been journaling throughout the time you've allotted to this experiment, check in at the end of it to see if it's taught you anything new about yourself and where your own walls are.

*WARNING: This exercise is <u>NOT</u> encouraging you to do anything that would cause mental or bodily harm or severe emotional distress to yourself or anyone else (Remember: Rule #1). Pick a topic, person, or activity that challenges what you've been taught, but don't engage with anything that causes your heart to seize up at the thought of encountering it. And definitely DO NOT engage with a person you fear may cause you harm without a professional intermediary such as a therapist, law enforcement, or a lawyer.

ALL TIED UP

In the archaic world, markets first appeared on the roads and borders that connected independent settlements. These ancient agoras offered citizens of different territories opportunities to exchange their goods and discover treasures from other lands. Thus, Trickster's dominion over boundaries evolved to include governance of exchange (such as market exchange), contracts, oaths, and other binding agreements. As a boundary binds a geographical area, a contract binds an individual, so Trickster's influence grew to cover binding and releasing in general.

Trickster embodies duality. After all, a guardian of the boundary would be the gatekeeper of both sides. Trickster's power of laying traps to bind us, then, also comes with the ability to effect our release. Not only can he catch us, he can also set us free.

On the Spiritual Path, Trickster's role in binding and releasing most commonly comes into play when considering our *attachments*. Defined as "joined, connected, bound," attachments are the people, things, and ideas we hold onto in life. The term "bound" is a word we often use to describe someone who is not free to exercise their own will, and this is just what our attachments can do to us. If we're not paying attention, they will rule our lives.

Most of us have many layers of attachments. It's easy to spot the ones that loom large—loved ones, life aspirations, or career ambitions, for example. We might even feel a bond with our favorite sofa. More surreptitious are the subtle attachments—those tangled up with our personality.

Identity attachments don't have to be big concepts like our religious affiliation or our political leanings (although these are legitimate examples). The most pernicious are often very specific ideas about ourselves, both positive and negative, that stick in our hearts like chewing gum in our hair.

We affix to the notion of ourselves as attractive, or compassionate, or spiritual, as good writers, or dutiful parents, or even just *young*. Perhaps someone we respect once made an admiring comment about our intelligence, prompting us to engage in behavior that reinforces and validates that idea. We might take Mensa quizzes or sign up for challenging intellectual classes. We may give our opinion more freely than if we thought our intelligence was suspect. Conversely, since the underside of attachment is fear of losing whatever we are attached to, we may do the opposite—shy away from intellectual pursuits completely, afraid they will topple our tenuous confidence in our own abilities. In their book *NurtureShock*,

Po Bronson and Ashley Merryman report how fifth-graders in a study employ such a strategy.

> "Researchers would take a single child out of the [fifth-grade] classroom for a non-verbal IQ test consisting of a series of puzzles...easy enough that all the children would do fairly well. Randomly divided into groups, some [students] were praised for their intelligence. Other students were praised for their effort. Then the students were given a choice of test for the second round. One choice was a test that would be more difficult than the first, but the researchers told the kids they'd learn a lot from attempting the puzzles. The other choice...was an easy test, just like the first. Of those praised for their effort, 90% chose the harder set of puzzles. Of those praised for their intelligence, a majority chose the easy test. The 'smart' kids took the cop-out."[15]

If we become attached to a personality trait within our power to maintain, we're likely to do everything we can to keep it. But if we're tied to an idea about ourselves we cannot control (intelligence, for example), we may avoid prospects that put this precious piece of our identity at risk.

In my blossoming youth, I had several boyfriends comment on the softness of my skin, and, embarrassingly enough, I grew attached to this idea—silly and shallow as it was. In aging, my skin has become less naturally soft, and I am chagrined at how much I have fretted over whether to start using lotion, buffing my skin, drinking more water, and so on. I have even avoided being touched when I think my skin is less than soft, affecting my romantic life.

Such is how a seemingly inconsequential attachment can influence how we live our lives and navigate our relationships. If we're bound by a

---

[15]   Po Bronson and Ashley Merryman, *NurtureShock: New Thinking About Children* (New York: Twelve, 2009), 14

collection of unseen attachments, it's nearly impossible to make objective decisions. Part of our Soulwork is recognizing the notions we hold on to that hinder our progress.

The flip side of Trickster's association with binding is his ability to liberate, to help us out of a jam, to highlight the escape clause in a contract, or aid our letting go of an old, unhelpful attachment. Trickster's power to release is metaphysical, working on a soul level, yet simultaneously literal and concrete.

One of my favorite stories of Trickster's emancipating powers comes from Dan Flores's book *Coyote America* and details how a Navajo tribe calls on Trickster directly to secure their freedom.

> "By 1864, some 8,000 Navajos had surrendered to the frontier army, only to find themselves condemned to incarceration in eastern New Mexico, three hundred miles from home. Their 'Long Walk' to the Bosque Redondo prison camp and four years imprisoned there under constant guard is a searingly painful chapter in Navajo history. But Navajos also recall how this episode ended. After years of pleading to return home...in 1868, the United States finally agreed to a treaty that gave the Navajos a reservation and allowed them to return to their homeland. In Navajo oral tradition, the act that accomplished this longed-for release was not negotiation or pleading. It was their ritual performance of a Coyote Way ceremony, which infused Navajo leaders with enough 'Coyote Power' to finally effect their release."[16]

Not only did Coyote's energy aid in releasing them from imprisonment, but the Navajo also came out of this episode securing a peace treaty (binding agreement) and a self-governing territory (geographical

---

[16] Dan Flores, *Coyote America: A Natural & Supernatural History* (New York: Basic Books, 2016), Amazon Digital Services, loc 864 of 4955, Kindle

boundary)—two other areas that fall under Trickster's jurisdiction. Obviously, the positive value of those last two items is subject to debate; without doubt, inequity was built into the current system. Even so, many cultural sub-groups across the world don't have *any* recognition or protection of their culture or rights, an unfortunate reality.

Although I don't have any Coyote ceremonies to share, I do know that we can use the lens of binding and releasing to look at our own lives and reflect on what ideas, people, places, and things keep us in bondage. The goal is not necessarily to force ourselves to release them, rather to be aware of how those bonds influence our behavior. Only when we are aware of them can we consciously *choose* which attachments to keep or let go.

Exercise: *Spend some time thinking about the <u>ideas</u> about yourself you are attached to. Do you think of yourself as intelligent, kind, hard-working? We can even be attached to negative ideas about ourselves if we think of ourselves as depressed, or lonely, or unappreciated, for example. Pick one self-identity you are bound to and reflect on the following:*

- *What are some things you do to protect this image of yourself?*
- *How do you react when one of these ideas is threatened? In other words, if you believe you are 'x' and someone suggests you are 'not-x' how would you react?*
- *Has there ever been a moment when you've had an idea of yourself challenged to the point you felt you had to change it?*
- *How does this attachment influence your life, and, now that you are conscious of it, would you choose to continue allowing it the same level of influence?*

HIDE AND SEEK

Who can see the border between Illinois and Indiana? Who can see the bindings of a sworn oath? Many boundaries and bindings are invisible to the naked eye. Thus, Trickster's guardianship expands to include what is hidden and revealed. On the Spiritual Path, Trickster can reveal the deep wounds, fears, and attachments we hide from ourselves so that we can heal and release them.

Besides deep soul wounds, secret insecurities, or fears, we might also obscure other aspects of our lives we don't want to see. We may reside in a wonderfully comfortable prison, for example, and not want to see it *as* a prison. We can only change what we grant ourselves access to. We don't need to alter everything we unearth, but awareness allows us to consciously choose.

After my husband left, I became the primary chef for myself and my two young daughters. They are selective eaters, so I limited myself to carb-heavy recipes with rice, pasta, and biscuits, thinking this would make our meals more palatable for them. I worried about gaining weight, especially with COVID restrictions, because I, too, consumed these carbs.

Yet over time I realized that the girls weren't really *eating* the carbohydrate-heavy foods. I had assumed that they liked them and acted on autopilot. But meal after meal, pasta and rice were left on the plate, and I ate more carbohydrate-heavy leftovers as a result.

I'm doing this to myself, I realized. *The kids aren't eating the pasta, rice, or even biscuits. Maybe I should just stop making them.*

So, I did. And I've dropped three pounds as a result. I could have just kept cooking the same things ad infinitum, but when I allowed myself to see that the reality wasn't matching my assumption, I could consciously make a change.

If we're interested in finding our hidden Soulwork, we can start by observing our own emotional reactions and automatic behaviors. If you've ever thought, *Why did I just do that?* It's an invitation to look closer—you might be hiding a fear or limiting belief from your conscious awareness.

With careful self-observation, patterns may emerge that lead us to a deeper understanding of what we're hiding. We can't resolve a problem until we find the root; otherwise, we're just addressing the symptoms. When we have a clearer picture of our Soulwork, we can apply our energy to resolving the underlying conditions that trigger our emotional overreactions and unhelpful unconscious behaviors.

Exercise: *Think of a time when you behaved a particular way and later wondered why. Give yourself space to reflect on what happened and how you felt at the time. See if related incidents come to mind in the following days and weeks.*

If nothing comes to mind, feedback also offers fertile territory for exploration. Write down a few pieces of uncomfortable feedback you've received from others.

Read aloud each piece of feedback individually, noticing your emotional response each time. Defensive? Thoughtful? Hurt? Dismissive? Angry?

Don't worry about analyzing or rationalizing the feedback—just write down what specific words, phrases, or ideas trigger you emotionally.

LOSING OUR WAY AND FINDING OURSELVES

From his guardianship over what is hidden and revealed, Trickster becomes authority over what is lost and found. This is yet another way that Trickster engages with us on the Spiritual Path. What I find and lose on the Path is frequently tied to a piece of Soulwork. With symbolic loss, once we master the lesson at hand, what went missing is either returned to us, or something new grows into the space left behind.

About a decade ago, I put together a spiritual development class and compiled a binder full of relevant readings, my own writing, and exercises. At the time, I suffered under a Dark Night of the Soul in my personal life and felt a bit lost on my Path. I searched for someone further along who could guide me through my current struggles. Unexpectedly, I came across a potential mentor, so I set up an appointment to discuss the idea with him.

Part of my trouble was that, thus far, I'd found meditation teachers, intuition coaches, mediums, shamans, and others willing to train in various spiritual development skills. But I hadn't yet found anyone who provided guidance on working through Soulwork or the Spiritual Path, specifically.

I combed our condo for that binder the whole morning. I planned to bring my work, hoping it would encourage him to take me on as a student. But it was as if the giant three-ring plastic folder had just *disappeared* in our tiny living space. I went to the meeting disheartened, and sadly it did not go as I had wished. My hoped-for guide turned out to be a leader in a new religious movement I wasn't sure I wanted to join. He invited me to meet the rest of their small group at an upcoming brunch. Unsure where this new Path would lead, but always willing to experiment, I agreed. Yet, I departed feeling more confused than ever.

The brunch gathering convinced me this group was not the right fit. I would just have to get through this rocky patch of my Path, having faith that my Relationship with the Universe would lead me in the right direction. Once my heart committed to this decision, I found my binder *exactly where I had left it* in the narrow gap between my bed and the bookcase I used for a nightstand. It was the only object there. I had been *so* sure I'd left the binder in that spot (it was the only place I ever put it) that I checked it *four times* the morning of my appointment but had only seen empty space. When I recognized the value of my own experience and allowed my intuition to guide me away from that group, my spiritual work was returned to me.

We can engage with symbolic loss in our lives by asking, *What is this loss teaching me?* Perhaps the answers aren't immediately obvious, but clarity may come if we let the question percolate in the background. (In compassion, I am not suggesting you take this approach with the loss of a loved one through tragedy or death; please use your own heart or a professional therapist as a guide in such treacherous terrain.)

Fortunately, it's not *just* loss that Trickster brings our way. Trickster also helps us *find*: find solutions to our problems, find our way, find our Soulwork, find ourselves.

One of my favorite anecdotes from Sonia Choquette's book *Walking Home*, demonstrates Trickster's playful influence over being lost and found, *especially* on the road. The book recounts Sonia's adventure walking the Camino de Santiago de Compostela. In Spanish, *Camino* means *way or route*, and the Camino de Santiago de Compostela is not just *any* road; it's a holy pilgrimage route, a causeway between Heaven and Earth.

Unsurprisingly, the book is peppered with Trickster-like antics in the exploits of Sonia and her fellow wayfarers. One memorable Trickster incident stood out above the rest, though. Sonia writes:

> "I entered a section of the Camino where everything seemed strange and magical and out of this world, and I found myself totally turned around. I couldn't find the arrows anywhere. I was lost.
>
> I continued on a bit farther and came to several forks in the road, a heavy mist in all directions. I was confused and didn't know where I was or which way to go.... Following my instincts, I took the Path to the left, where I eventually came upon...a house with an open door, so I called out. Then I boldly walked in, hoping to ask for directions....
>
> Inside was an older, scruffy, Spanish-speaking man... who invited me into his kitchen to have coffee....I thanked him and declined, saying I just needed to get back to the Camino, but he shook his head and said that

I was brought to him by the Camino for a reason and I should stop and rest. Seeing the light in his clear dark eyes, I knew that it was true."[17]

What follows is a meaningful revelation and profoundly cathartic experience for Sonia. The nature of her happening upon the house has all the signs of Trickster's whimsical intervention: obscuring mists, crossroads, a lack of proper signage. This place must be *found*. It's not a stop on the map.

Ironically, in several chapters of the book, Sonia prays *not* to get lost. Obviously, she wants to avoid being *physically* lost as she walks the pilgrimage route, but, as a Spirit worker, Sonia also wishes to avoid being *spiritually* lost. She doesn't want to "lose her way." It is the hallmark of Trickster that here is an instance where she does, in fact, get lost—and yet she finds the healing she may have needed most on this journey.

Even as a reader, I can *feel* Trickster's presence in these moments: walking with Sonia, turning her around like a child playing Pin the Tail on the Donkey, reminding her to look with her heart instead of her eyes, and ultimately leading her to a moment of beautiful truth and connection.

Exercise: *Reflect on a time you have lost or found something (it doesn't have to be a physical thing, it can be an idea about yourself, for example, but please don't force yourself to relive the trauma of losing a loved one if you're not ready for something like that).*

- *Was there anything that felt symbolic about the loss or find?*
- *Did it teach you anything?*
- *Have you ever "found" something or someone (or even a class) that seemed like a gift or a happy accident? If so, how did it impact your life?*

---

[17] Choquette, Sonia *Walking Home* (Hay House Inc., September 30, 2014), 308

Synthesis

I introduce each of Trickster's lenses in an order that allows us to see how they expand and evolve from his original role as guardian of the boundary. In working through our Soulwork, though, these lenses operate more synergistically. For example, Trickster's role in what is hidden and revealed can help us discover our boundaries and the attachments that bind us. Likewise, Trickster's role in finding and releasing can help us locate ways to liberate ourselves from attachments and wounds we no longer want to hold onto.

If we're crossing a boundary into uncharted territory, whether that's in our personal life, through our technical work, our artistic efforts, or even in our own minds, it's helpful to be aware that Trickster traps may be lying in wait in his other areas of influence. We may be hiding something from ourselves. Or, we may need to evaluate what might limit our success. We can more deftly traverse tricky terrain when we toggle through all the lenses each time we advance on a boundary.

We can also work in-depth with a single lens, though. We may *find* a new creative direction or *hide* a precious project we're working on until we're ready to share. Ultimately, in applying the four lenses of Trickster, we learn to approach obstacles from many angles and increase our pace of learning. The more we work with Trickster energy, the less conscious thought it requires. Trickster's lenses offer a different way of *seeing* the world that becomes our natural method of engaging with our environment.

Exercise: *Think of a current challenge you are facing—it can be personal, work-related, in the home and family space, or a relationship issue. Ask yourself the following questions about your challenge. Journal the answers and see what comes up:*

- *Are any boundaries preventing progress? Are any boundaries being crossed? What boundaries? Whose boundaries? Are these boundaries visible and obvious or unseen?*
- *Is there anything binding me (or anyone else) in the situation? Am I holding onto any attachments here? (Including attachment to outcome.) Is anyone else holding onto any attachments? (It's always good practice to look at ourselves first before widening the lens to include others.)*
- *Do I need to release anything? If so, what? How might I let it go?*
- *What am I hiding from in this situation? Is there any knowledge that might be hidden from* me *in this situation? Am I hiding anything from anyone else? If so, why? What might be the impact if whatever is hidden is revealed?*
- *Has anything been lost? Have I lost something? Has someone else lost something? (This doesn't have to be a physical item; it can be a loss of identity, sense of self, safety, financial security, even the loss of a dream.) Do I need to allow myself to grieve whatever has been lost as a method of release? Or have compassion for someone else's experience?*

4

GEARING UP

Equipping for Our Journey

We don't embark on a hiking trip without any gear, and we shouldn't go on a spiritual journey ill-equipped either. This section will introduce some of the tools we'll use along the way. In our case, the tools are conceptual rather than concrete but critical to safely walking the Path.

BEGINNER'S MIND

Adopting a *Beginner's Mind* means that whatever previous experience we bring to the Path (and to this book), we benefit most from approaching the material as if it were new. This does not mean we forget all we have learned already, just that we release ourselves from its hold and avoid using it as a form of judgment until we've given the new material a chance to digest and integrate into our consciousness.

In the past, I have sometimes been guilty of building walls around what I already know. I can't tell you how many times I've read a book about spirituality and felt a rising wave in my abdomen, thinking, *I've been doing this for over a decade; I know this already.* While it's great to feel proud of and honor the work we've already done, constraining ourselves to its limits inhibits growth.

Several years ago, As I traveled through the pages of Alberto Villoldo's book *The Four Insights*, I thought, *I already know this stuff.* Nevertheless, I kept going. I had heard of the concept of Beginner's Mind[18] in an advertorial around that same time and recognized that I could benefit from applying it to reading Villoldo's work. *Yes,* I told myself, *I know a lot about spirituality already, but let's see if this book has something for me anyway.* So, instead of shutting down, I opened up, and in the pages within, I found a story that vaulted me to a new level of understanding.

Remember when I mentioned coming into work like a rainbow and leaving like a thundercloud? Villoldo's book helped me understand why. In it, he tells of studying under a Peruvian shaman. The two travel around the Amazon together and, one day, come to a village that had requested the shaman's help relieving a long-suffered drought. After dining with the villagers, the master shaman shut himself up in a little hut with no human contact and little sustenance. Three days later, to the delight of the villagers, it began to rain.

Villoldo recounts his master's explanation of the experience, "when we arrived at the village, he noticed that it was out of [alignment][19]. It was so out of balance, in fact, that *he* became out of balance, too. He couldn't do anything until he went back into [alignment] when he did, so did the village, and the rains came."[20]

---

[18] Now that I am going back over my sources, I realize that Alberto Villoldo *also* talks about Beginner's Mind in his book *The Four Insights*, although I had seen the advertorial before getting to that point in the book. Another one of those coincidences!

[19] The actual word Villoldo uses here is *ayni* which he translates as 'right relation-ship to nature'. For conciseness, I translate it here as "alignment."

[20] Alberto Villoldo, PH.D., *The Four Insights: Wisdom, Power, and Grace of the Earthkeepers* (Hay House, 2006), 162

Tears welled in my eyes as I read this. I had thought my fifteen years of meditation and spiritual practice would allow me to easily maintain my equilibrium and positive energy throughout a hectic workday in a building full of hundreds of stressed-out people. (The building actually contained well over a thousand people, but hopefully they weren't all stressed out!) If walking into an unbalanced village could throw a master shaman out of alignment, my expectations of myself were *way too high*.

Not only was realizing this a tremendous relief, but seeing the issue allowed me to actually work on the problem. First, I could release my self-judgment and revise my expectations of myself. One of the biggest inhibitors to our own happiness can be unrealistic beliefs about what we can or should be able to handle. Intentionally letting those go lifts a crushing weight off us. Free from self-judgment, I redirected my focus to wondering what I could do to re-balance myself during the day. I could take some time for meditation over lunch, for example, or add some items that spark my sense of humor and play to my workspace (like a Far Side desk calendar) for a quick pick-me-up in moments of stress.

Even implementing all those strategies, I still wasn't able to leave as a rainbow, but I *did* manage to only slide into a light drizzle. Because I had amended my expectations, though, I could be blissfully proud of that achievement instead of disappointed in myself.

When we are drawn to books, movies, classes, or people, they usually have something to teach us. It may not always be what we think it is, and it may not be what we *want* to learn, but there tends to be a reason. Our openness toward what we *can* learn will usually determine how much we *do* learn. If we approach a new experience with the idea that we know it all already, we may miss the critical lesson.

With the tool of Beginner's Mind, Trickster teaches us to release our attachments to what we already know. We resist the impulse to form initial judgments based on pre-existing ideas and allow ourselves to learn. "Yes, I may know a lot, I have experienced a lot," we acknowledge, "but let's pretend I don't know anything at all and see if this shows me a new way to look at something familiar."

Instead of a bouncer at the door of our consciousness, we're a welcoming host throwing a neighborhood party. Of course, we won't be besties with everyone we meet, but we can engage our joyful curiosity by at least getting to know the ideas that show up. And maybe, just maybe, we'll meet an idea that completely changes our life.

Exercise: *Ask yourself what you already know that might impact how you approach the information in this book or your Spiritual Path experience?*

Write down what comes up in your journal so you can revisit later if needed.

TAI CHI FIST

In my late teens and early twenties, I studied Tai Chi, a slow-form Chinese martial art combining energy work and defense training. As I mentioned in the introduction, I first discovered I could feel my own energy—my first direct spiritual encounter—through Tai Chi. One concept from those early days that has been valuable throughout my journey is "Tai Chi fist."

When we make a Tai Chi fist, we imagine clutching a small bird. We want to hold the bird firmly enough that it won't fly away, but not so tightly that we crush it. Where Beginner's Mind provides us with a framework for approaching new information, Tai Chi fist teaches us how to handle the information we decide to hang on to. I have returned to this concept many times on my own path as a way to manage ideas.

We come across many new concepts as we walk the Spiritual Path. We want to keep collecting new knowledge, as this is how we build understanding and evolve our thinking. While ideas, approaches, and practices serve us well, we benefit from holding onto them, using them actively, and engaging with them frequently. However, an idea or practice that once resonated very strongly might be outgrown a few years later. We will find some concepts and techniques that we simply need to release. If we hold onto a former mental model too tightly, we could keep ourselves stuck when we most need to grow.

With Tai Chi fist, we may hold the bird tightly enough to prevent it from flying away, but the hidden truth is that we will not trap a bird in our fists forever. When we're ready, because we haven't crushed it, we can set the bird free. If we cultivate a healthy relationship *with* ideas rather than an attachment *to* them, we can open our fists with a spirit of gratitude and release old ideas as we grow into new ones.

Although I started using the idea of Tai Chi fist on the earliest days of my journey, a dozen years before I found Trickster, the concept aligns beautifully with Trickster's role in binding and releasing. Part of navigating our Spiritual Path is discerning when to hold onto a person, a practice, a notion, or a situation and when to let go.

For the first decade of walking my Spiritual Path, I did not believe in a cohesive soul, a unique self. I figured our perception of the individual soul came from an attachment to the identity we create throughout life. At death, I envisioned our personal energy rejoining the collective energy of the Universe, no longer separate and distinct.

In 2011, I attended a meditation class focused on healing others through energy work. For one exercise, class attendees partnered up, and the instructor directed one partner to approach the other without touching them, advancing to the edge of their energy field. I had been meditating with my own energy for years but was floored to feel the tingly tickle of *another* person's energy in my field.

Several weeks later, while walking back to the office from lunch, I unexpectedly felt that same sensation. This time experiencing it *inside my body*: butterflies fluttering simultaneously in my heart, diaphragm, and stomach. Unable to focus through the distraction, I had to sit down and wait for it to pass. I wondered if I might be pregnant. Had I been feeling the presence of the baby's energy, or soul, in my chakras? A test two weeks later confirmed my condition.

The prenatal energy in my field hadn't been "loose" energy; it had been a defined presence. Should I hold onto my concept of a non-cohesive soul or allow for the possibility that a distinct soul might exist outside the body? Obviously, I can't claim to know the objective truth, but remembering Tai Chi fist enabled me to release my old mental construct. Rather than forcing the new experience to fit my old framework, I opened to a new way of thinking.

Exercise: *Explore within yourself any practices or mental models that may have initially catalyzed your growth that now, potentially, hold you back? Are you ready to let go of these to allow something new in its place?*

EMOTIONAL RELEASE

In Douglas Adams's book *The Hitchhiker's Guide to the Galaxy*, there's a famous phrase that echoes throughout the book: *When you're traveling the Universe, always remember to bring your towel.* I can't help but laugh and think that the corresponding version for traveling our *inner* Universe is: *Always remember to bring your tissue.* If the primary goal of the Spiritual Path is development of the soul, then we will sometimes (probably more often than we'd *like*) discover things on our path that are uncomfortable—about our world, about our relationships, and about ourselves.

When we suppress our emotions, we trap ourselves in a prison of our own making. In practicing Emotional Release, we allow ourselves to express whatever comes up through an outlet that feels comfortable to us (and, of course, doesn't harm anyone else). I've already mentioned a few revelations that brought tears to my eyes. Allowing ourselves to cry is an excellent form of Emotional Release.

We're not limited to waterworks, though—art, music, writing, dance, or any other avenue of expression functions just as well. We can even Emotionally Release through kickboxing, exercise, or pummeling a punching bag. My Emotional Release process has sometimes involved crying while dancing. (Which is why I often do it alone.)

There is no mental component to Emotional Release. We're not interested in naming or figuring out what we're feeling. At no point are we trying to reason with, rationalize, or judge what emerges. Allow your emotions to express themselves, as they are, until they are done. If you are an artist or a writer and cannot use those mediums without treating the output as "work," find another mechanism for release.

Once we have worked through what has come up, any stress, tension, or negativity we have built up from carrying those emotions will disappear, unblocking the path to further evolve.

We can use *Emotional Release* on the Spiritual Path whenever we like. When we don't allow enough space for processing our emotions, we might feel scattered. Our emotions might erupt in destructive ways, creating a mess we need to clean up after the storm.

Suppose I hadn't allowed myself to cry, uninhibited, when I discovered my role in the fractured relationship with my then-mother-in-law. I might have withdrawn, instead, into shame or defensiveness, making the situation worse. Withdrawal would also have hurt my relationship with my then-husband. Because I had allowed myself to grieve in facing this unflattering part of myself, I could pivot toward pride in finding and navigating it. Free to release any self-judgment over the matter, my focus shifted to mending the relationship. As a result, it significantly improved.

Exercise: *Explore how you Emotionally Release? If nothing comes to mind, ask yourself when you're most likely to feel your emotions stir. It could be listening to music, watching a poignant film, dancing, playing an instrument,* *writing, singing, drawing, painting, or anything—even running or playing a sport.*

Record your thoughts in your journal. Next time you feel a welling up of emotion, take some time to do an Emotional Releasing activity.

If your emotions never stir, that's good to know and ruminate on as you proceed on this journey.

ATTENTION

Attention may seem like an odd tool to mention on an expedition into the wilderness of our souls, but consider how bad an *actual* hike can go if we're not paying attention. We might stumble over a bush, get lost, or even walk off a ledge if we're not mindful of where we are.

Attention may be even more critical on the Spiritual Path. At least on a hike we have some idea of *what* we're supposed to pay attention to: the trail, the map, the sights, wildlife, avoiding a stumble over rocks or roots. Since we're on the Spiritual Path all the time and must walk it in tandem with our practical existence, we may be unclear about *what* we need to attend to and *when*.

Even if the Universe is hitting us over the head with a message, we won't "get it" if our minds are focused on what happened at home in the morning, or how we wish we hadn't said *that* in today's meeting, or what we're having for dinner. We miss guidance if we're not attending to the right things. And yet we can't pay attention to *every*thing *all* the time.

So how *do* we know where to direct our attention?

We can think of Attention as one of Trickster's secret names, and we have to *pay* him to show us the important stuff. He is the governor of exchange, after all, as well as our Spiritual Path guide. Joking aside, the truth is that we receive signals from the Universe through our energy field. The next part of the book covers quieting the mind, meditation, and developing our energy sensitivity, three skills to help you increase awareness of energetic signals. Quieting the mind coupled with meditation helps us cultivate the space necessary to pay attention, and our energy directs us to meaningful guidance.

Think for a minute: What determines where we look and why? Our eyes are constantly moving, passing over the scenery, resting on a seemingly random object. Yes, sometimes we deliberately *look* at something, but what about all those other times? What about when we're just walking down the street? Or sitting in a lobby?

These days, our focus is often consumed by our mobile devices. Yet there are still moments when our attention drifts, our eyes land on an object, our ears detect a sound, our noses pick up a smell. All of these are opportunities to receive guidance. Any moment where we're open to receiving input, the Universe, our Guides, or our soul can communicate with us.

While driving home from an intuition workshop, for example, I asked my Guides what I needed to do next. My eyes instantly caught sight of a giant billboard on the side of the road. All it said, in giant green letters, was "GROW." Another example: the time I left a takeout restaurant, wrestling with uncertainty that I would ever find success with my book, worried that I was just wasting my already scarce time. My eyes fell on the back of a T-shirt worn by one of the diners. "Doubt kills more dreams than failure ever could," it read.

Indeed.

This book is full of stories like these; they're all brought to you by the skill of Attention. I received the guidance because I noticed what my eyes fell on. If I had been too wrapped up in my thoughts, I would have missed the message entirely.

Exercise: *Take a day to notice where you direct your attention most often. Is it work? Is it social media? Is it the news? Is it family responsibilities? What*

and how much is giving your attention to these things giving back to you?
What is missing your attention? What are you neglecting?

HUMOR AND PLAY

Last but far from least in our bag of tricks are humor and play—possibly the most necessary tools of all. Both humor and play are closely associated with Trickster's areas of influence. We might *find* humor in a situation, and comedy can release us from the bindings of tension and grief. Both animals and humans use play to test boundaries and learn the skills needed to maneuver in a high-stakes world.

In his book *Ha! The Science of When We Laugh, and Why,* author Scott Weems identifies humor as "the social or psychological working through of ideas that are not easily handled by our conscious minds."[21]

The discoveries that trip us up when walking the Spiritual Path are definitely ideas "not easily handled by our conscious minds." Thus, humor is a natural companion on our trip. When our Spiritual Path gets intense, humor keeps us sane. Humor relieves anxiety and creates openness within us to find new solutions and bridge divides. My ability to laugh at myself and my circumstances has been invaluable when facing adversity in life, especially when navigating Soulwork.

We don't even have to laugh *about* the specific circumstances causing us stress to find relief from them in humor. In one of my favorite Trickster stories from the Norse tradition, the gods, somewhat accidentally, kill storm giant Thiassi. His daughter approaches them, furious and devastated over her father's death.

---

[21]   Scott Weems, *Ha! The Science of When We Laugh and Why* (New York: Basic Books, 2014), Amazon Digital Services, loc. 107 of 4245

"[Chief god] Odin spoke kindly to her, saying, 'We will do honor to your father by putting his eyes in the sky, where they will always shine as two bright stars, and the people of Midgard will remember Thiassi whenever they look up at the night and see the two twinkling lights. Besides this, we will also give you gold and silver.' But Skadi, thinking money could never repay for the loss of her father, was still angry. Loki looked at her stern face, and he said to himself, 'If only we can make Skadi laugh, she will be more ready to agree to the plan,' and he began to think of some way to amuse her. Taking a long cord, he tied it to a goat; it was an invisible cord...and Loki himself held the other end of it. Then he began to dance and caper about, and the goat had to do just what Loki did. It really was such a funny sight that all the gods shouted with laughter, and even poor, sorrowful Skadi had to smile. When the [gods] saw this, they proposed another plan...."[22]

Through the power of humor, Loki releases Skadi from her grief and creates an opening for transformative healing to begin. Even chief god Odin, with his promises of stars in the sky, couldn't do that.

The sibling of humor is, of course, play. Adopting a playful mindset allows us to engage experimentally in the world and encourages us to step out of our comfort zone.

Weems notes a University of Maryland study where researchers asked participants to solve the Duncker candle insight task. Given a candle, a box of tacks, and matches, subjects are asked to attach the candle to the wall so that it doesn't drip wax on the floor. Before attempting the puzzle, though, subjects had to engage in one of five pre-task activities: watching a compilation of funny bloopers, watching a five-minute documentary

---

[22]   Mabel H. Cummings and Mary H. Foster, *Asgard Stories Tales from Norse Mythology* (Book on Demand Ltd., 2013), 73

on Nazi concentration camps, watching a math film, eating a candy bar while relaxing, or exercising for two minutes.

The solution to the challenge requires thinking outside the box. Only 27% of participants overall configured the items correctly. "In fact, no group of subjects performed better than 30%—with one exception. The subjects who were shown the funny bloopers succeeded at a rate of 58%."[23]

Of course, it's only speculation as to why this happened. One reasonable explanation, though, is that watching other people commit embarrassing "bloopers" helped those subjects release self-consciousness about trying a solution that might make them look silly. Sometimes, on the Spiritual Path, we feel ridiculous following a particular piece of guidance. Treating these moments on the path with the spirit of play helps us tentatively tiptoe through this murky territory rather than freezing up in fear.

Sonia Choquette tells a story of receiving guidance that she needed to get on a different flight while waiting at the airport with her family to board their plane to Paris. Meanwhile, in her physical surroundings, everything seemed fine. Gamely following her intuition, Sonia faced off with an incredulous, hassled gate attendant to make the seemingly absurd request for her family of four to be rerouted, last minute.

The flight attendant blustered in irritation, trying to brush Sonia off, when suddenly, to the surprise of both, an announcement came through the intercom that the flight would be canceled due to a mechanical problem. Sonia got her family's tickets first of all the passengers, and they raced to their new gate before chaos descended on the dismayed airline staff.

If we take ourselves too seriously to risk looking stupid in following our guidance, we can't take advantage of all the energetic information available to us. We need to be lighthearted enough to be willing to say, "I know this sounds crazy, but...."

Humor and play also fill our hearts with joy, recharging our batteries with much-needed energy when we're deep in a quagmire of our own Soulwork. After a tumultuous session of Emotional Release or navigating a particularly tricky piece of Soulwork, reward yourself with some well-earned humor and play. In the most challenging moments, these help keep us going strong.

Exercise: *Where/When have you been too serious? Why? What do you find impossible to laugh about and why? What areas of your life could benefit from more humor and play?*

- *Start a list in your journal (devote an entire page to it) of things that make you laugh. At minimum, find five to seven shows, books, cartoon clips, or media clips that provoke your own mirth reliably. Add to this list when old things come to mind or when you find new ones. Feel free to jot down actual gut-busting events that happened in your life.*
- *Make a separate list on a separate page devoted to what you like to do for "play." It might be a sport that's been a long-standing part of your life, but stay in the space of what truly brings you joy versus just competitive satisfaction. It may help to think of activities you loved to do as a child: Sledding? Skating? Ping Pong? Climbing Trees? Coloring? It could even be, simply, trying new things.*

5

TRAIL NOTES

A Last Bit of Advice Before We Set Off

TIMING

We live in a world framed by twenty-four-hour news and on-demand social media. We watch the world spin around us at a seemingly faster pace than ever before. We might finish reading a book in a matter of hours or days, leading us to believe that we should get through the exercises and material equally fast. The Spiritual Path is not like that. Although I have certainly had sudden breakthroughs, those epiphanies were fed by weeks, months, sometimes years of significant background work.

This book represents twenty-five years of Soulwork compressed into a little over two hundred pages. Some lessons, described in a paragraph or a handful of pages, took me years to sort through. Please remember this on your journey. I chose not to do this book in a "weekly" format because I rarely follow preset timelines when I read books, and I have no idea what your pace will be. My recommendation is to read the book straight through. If it feels right, try all the exercises when you come across them, but avoid getting stuck in a particular place. If a specific practice isn't working for you, skip it and move on. When you've finished the book, you can decide what you want to return to.

It is also okay *not* to finish the book. Joseph Campbell's *The Hero with a Thousand Faces* and Huston Smith's *The World's Religions* were two of the most influential books on my initial Path. I've gone back to them multiple times. I still revere them today. And, even after all these years, I'm not sure I finished either one. We accelerate learning on the Path by finding "jumping-off" points. A nugget of information to start with that leads us in a new direction. Thus, I give you my permission to leave this book unfinished. You don't need my authorization, obviously, but I give it freely and happily. You are on your journey, not mine. Take whatever you need from what I've learned and let the rest go.

All I ask of you on your Spiritual Path and with your Soulwork is that you don't give up: *just keep going.*

BE YOUR OWN BAROMETER

Sometimes, when we encounter a spiritual practice that has worked wonders for others but leaves us unmoved, we beat ourselves up about it. We might think there's something wrong with us, or we're not doing it right. We may even conclude that we're just not meant to have a spiritual experience. Our Soulwork is specific to us, though, and the key to someone else's self-actualization may not be what unlocks our own.

Thus, we need to be, or become, our own barometer on the Path.

At first glance, this seems counterintuitive. After all, don't we seek help from teachers *because* they have mastered a skill that we haven't? Absolutely. We profit from the wisdom of those who have gone before. But, the veteran yoga teacher won't have to deal with our pulled tendon the following week. The inspirational life coach won't have to recover a depleted bank balance from us "investing in our dream." Almost all teachers we meet along the Path will have the best intentions at heart. But they, too, expect us to set and know our own boundaries.

When we follow the instructions of an expert, we need to listen to our innermost selves first; our bodies, hearts, and souls. We shift from blindly obeying the words of a master to retaining ownership of our own journey. We try a technique to see if it works for us.

Of course, we can be resistant to our own growth, and fear of pain or discomfort could turn us away from a powerfully transformative practice. Therein lies the challenge of this simple but not easy lesson. We negotiate between the boundaries of comfort and growth throughout our adventure on the Spiritual Path. The fear that protects our soul wounds from exposure is the same fear that protects us from genuine harm. Even after twenty-five years walking the Path, it's not always easy for me to tell in which situation I find myself. Take heart, though; if we miss an opportunity for growth, another will present itself.

Sometimes when we feel internal resistance, we need to experiment a bit to determine whether a particular practice is a good fit for our journey. My advice for beginners on the Path is to be very conscious of the line between discomfort and danger. Avoid techniques that feel *too* uncomfortable at first. As you gain skill at navigating the nebulous territory of spiritual development, you will build trust in your own discernment.

ENJOY WHERE YOU ARE

One bright fall morning, as I pulled my red Prius between the parallel lines of a parking spot on my way to an event, a midsize maple tree decked in vibrant autumnal glory beckoned me over. I noticed that every leaf on the tree seemed to be in a different state of transformation, from the verdant green of summer to the fiery hues of fall. Each leaf sported a different combination of the season's colors, dazzling in its precise state of meta-morphosis. Yet, every leaf contributed to the overall beauty of the tree.

Sometimes, we get caught up in comparing our journey to the journeys of others. Or we evaluate where we are in relation to where we think we should be. You are beautiful right where you are on your journey. As am I. As are we all.

Focusing on what we don't have, where we aren't yet, or where we used to be can pull us away from enjoying where we are.

About ten years into my Spiritual journey, I begin to wonder why I was no longer in the blissful state of euphoria that characterized my first few years on the Path. I wanted to know what I was doing wrong that I couldn't seem to get "back there." Following a particularly poignant moment of self-defeat, I realized that unfavorably comparing my current state to my previous one prevented me from fully engaging with my present. My Guides very lovingly reminded me that I had grown into a completely different person in those ten years. I had been in a delightful place at the start of my journey, but the person I had grown into was also worth celebrating, the difference between a fresh grape and a fine wine.

Sometimes, it's challenging to see the beauty of where we are because of our surrounding circumstances. There are moments when even a small smile is too much to ask of ourselves. Yet even in our darkest days, when the most difficult emotions let up for a bit, we can find sparks of love, comfort, joy, beauty, or maybe just peace. We might find enjoyment in snuggling a soft blanket against our skin or the gentle encirclement of a hug from a friend. We might find solace in something as small as the sudden burst of sunshine after a summer rain, lighting up emerald leaves against the dark wet bark of the trees.

Enjoying where we are doesn't mean we have to find joy in every single second. Rather, it's a recognition that what we're learning at this moment on our adventure has value. Whatever state of growth or transformation we're in contributes to who we are now and who we are becoming.

Don't worry about where anyone else is on their journey, and don't worry about where you are. You are exactly where you're meant to be right now. As much as you can, enjoy it.

PART 2

Reach Out, Touch Faith

Initiating Contact with the Universe

6

THE SIGNAL

Letting the Universe Know We're Serious

We might label the impetus that pulled you into this book, that has kept you reading to this point, *the Call*. In Joseph Campbell's best-selling book *The Hero with a Thousand Faces*, he discusses the Hero's Journey in mythology and folklore—coining the phrase, *"the Call to Adventure."*

The Call speaks to a wish that bubbles up from the soul—a longing to venture beyond mundane existence. Hearing and answering the Call is, in itself, worthy of applause. After all, many simply ignore it. Yet, it is only the first step on the journey.

When we make the conscious decision to engage with our Soulwork, we are ready for the second step: a direct signal of our intent to the Universe. Although I didn't realize it initially, in March of 1997, I sent up my own flare for help.

Studying abroad in England my freshman year, separated from the life I had always known by an ocean and time, I felt lost and confused on my current life path. It was in this slightly tormented state that I stumbled upon an old English church on a crisp spring afternoon. There wasn't anything particularly significant or unique about it—undoubtedly, there were dozens like it dotting the countryside. I hardly remember enough to form a sufficient description: a cavernous interior—dark wood, dark brick. In contrast, draped over a statue in front of the altar, bathed in sunlight, was a net peppered with colorful paper fish covered in writing. On a table nearby lay a pencil and a basket full of similar fish, empty of wishes and prayers.

I stared at the ink drying on the pink paper fish in my hand, so small it barely stretched across my palm. On its tiny body, I had scrawled four simple words: *Help Beth Find God.* Moisture accumulated in the corners of my eyes, everything that led to this moment pressing on me from behind: a long and heavy trailing shadow.

I can't pinpoint precisely when I started walking my Spiritual Path. A year of meditation preceded that moment on the stone floor of a church whose name I can't even remember. I choose this memory as the beginning, though, because it's the point where I was brave enough to admit just how lost I was—the point where I recognized the need to ask for directions. I put my heart on paper and my faith in the unknown that day as I took my next step into the future.

Luckily, you don't have to be as lost as I was to send your own signal to the Universe. Your gesture can be as simple as stating your intentions, "I want to begin my spiritual journey." You can write it as the first line in a journal you dedicate to walking the Spiritual Path. The words you use and how you ritualize them are entirely up to you.

Highlighting our intentions to the Universe aligns our energy and the energy of the Universe toward our goal. Our signal to the Universe must be clear, intentional, and serious. By *clear*, I mean not cluttered with fears or hidden agendas, such as a subconscious desire to confirm one's own skepticism or a secret hope to escape the challenges of life. Our signal will be best received by the Universe when we do it *intentionally*, reflecting a pure desire for connection in our hearts.

I cringe a bit, using the word *serious* to describe communication with the Universe. We tend to think of "serious" as stodgy and without joy when our Relationship with the Universe is often characterized by a jubilant feeling of connection and peace. Instead, I refer to the definition of serious: "being in earnest, sincere, not trifling," as well as "requiring thought, concentration, or application."[24] Even when approaching our Relationship with the Universe in whimsy and wonder, our engagement should reflect the characteristics of seriousness noted above.

For those who don't feel comfortable speaking or writing, sending a signal doesn't have to take form in words. Drawing, painting, sculpting, and musical composition are perfectly acceptable ways to signal to the Universe we're ready to *officially* start our journey.

Exercise: *How would you send your signal to the Universe? Think about what you would do, how you would do it, and whether you are ready now.*

Thinking about how we would signal our intentions to the Universe can be a point of self-observation. Would we feel self-conscious saying it aloud? Might someone overhear us? What if someone reads our journal? What would they think? The stronger our reservations are, the more likely they will prevent us from experimenting on our Spiritual Path.

Have you already sent your signal to the Universe at some point in the past? Write, draw, or speak the memory into a recorder to consciously cement that moment of your journey. Connect it with where you are now.

---

[24] dictionary.com

COMMITMENT

Since our signal to the Universe is a commitment, it's worth touching on that subject before we go further.

Who *hasn't* made a reckless commitment in a moment of duress?

> *Please <insert divine authority>, get me out of this mess and I'll never drink/smoke/bite my nails/lie/go home with a stranger/whatever/again.*

How often, when we actually *do* find ourselves out of the mess, does that promise seem…silly? Unachievable? Who expects us to keep a promise like that? If the harmful habit we are trying to kick is pervasive, or the positive practice we wish to instill has many barriers, how often do we keep that promise?

I know my answer: not as often as I'd like.

Those promises and commitments seem less pertinent when we're back in our comfort zone. Why does the Universe care if I drink soda? Or alcohol? Or smoke? Yet our Relationship with the Universe is as much about building trust as any physical relationship we have. If we never kept our commitments to friends or loved ones, what would those relationships be like?

We have every reason to believe the Universe pays attention to the promises we make. Remember that Trickster governs binding and releasing. When we bind *ourselves,* Trickster takes note. Breaking a vow erodes trust between ourselves and the Universe, hindering our journey. Luckily, both Trickster and the Universe care more about how much weight we give our commitments than *what* we commit to.

Don't stop making commitments; they are a vital component of our Relationship with the Universe and fundamental to our Soulwork.

However, we benefit from being more thoughtful and realistic about what we pledge.

If we make commitments we are willing and able to fulfill, they strengthen our Relationship. For example, we might promise that every time we receive a message from the Universe, we will record it—in a notebook, on a sticky note, on a napkin, or even via a voice recording on our phone. If we don't want to commit to recording the sign on the spot, we can charge ourselves with documenting it before bed that night. That is a *meaningful* vow that shouldn't be difficult to fulfill.

CEMENTING OUR COMMITMENT

Our mindful commitments indicate to the Universe that we respect our journey and approach it with serious intent. The signal we send to the Universe that we are ready to actively walk our Spiritual Path is a commitment to honor the Call, be open to guidance, and find and engage with our Soulwork.

Our assurance only sticks, though, if we uphold that commitment through practice. Thus, this section of the book presents three essential skills we can practice regularly to cement our commitment. They are: quieting the mind, meditating, and developing our energy sensitivity.

Why start with these?

We receive advice from the Universe through our energy field. Building our energy awareness increases the likelihood we'll notice when the Universe or our Guides are seeking our attention. If our mind is wound up about something, we're likely to miss this assistance entirely. Quieting the mind minimizes distracting thoughts that impede our ability to notice subtle "tugs" on our energy field.

Meditation is a single word for a multitude of practices that help us approach our Soulwork. By helping us develop a remote vantage point through which to observe the self, meditation provides an avenue to practice the skills needed to discover our Soulwork.

Exercise: *Think of two to three spiritual commitments you are tempted to make and write them down. Ask yourself if you are really willing and able to meet those commitments. Don't make them yet!*

Revisit them as you go through this section of the book and see how your feelings around them develop. Assess whether you would change them. After waiting at least a few days, ask yourself if you are ready to make these commitments.

7

Hear a Pin Drop

Quieting the Mind

You might wonder why quieting the mind has its own chapter. After all, the next chapter covers meditation, and isn't that what meditation is supposed to do? But training the mind to be quiet is a skill in its own right. Developing that skill in tandem with creating a meditation practice can actually be more challenging than learning to quiet the mind first and then *applying* that skill during meditation. For most of us, it's easier to focus on one thing at a time.

In mindfulness meditation, guidance for beginners is often to *watch* the thoughts. "Let them come and let them go." These are wise words. It's unhelpful to judge ourselves when ideas arise during meditation. Forcing our thoughts to leave distracts us from being present with ourselves. Learning to let our thoughts come and go during meditation is a worthwhile skill to develop. And practice redirecting our thoughts to the breath when we're distracted has cross-over benefits in our daily life. However, it is *possible* to quiet the mind, and my meditation practice is more satisfying and fruitful when my mental noise calms.

A quiet mind provides open space for guidance to come in from the Universe. Energetic indicators are subtle, like the ticking of the wall clock we only notice when no one else is around. If our mind is busier than a travel terminal, we won't hear whispers from the Universe.

So how *do* we quiet the mind?

Let me ask this: *Is your mind noisy right now?* Chances are it isn't, and neuroscientific study provides insight on why. To explain, we need to introduce two neural networks that often come up in meditation studies: the default mode network and the task-positive network.

The default mode network is responsible for some critical aspects of humanity, such as self-reflection and empathy. Without it, we wouldn't be able to learn from our mistakes or feel compassion for others. However, when the default mode network is *too* active, it can cause mind-wandering, obsessing over the past and future, and over-analyzing our own or others' actions. Unsurprisingly, excessive default mode network activity is associated with depression and anxiety disorders.

For many of us, the default mode network is active, often, throughout the day—when we're driving, sitting in a waiting room, standing in line, or performing other routine tasks that don't require our total concentration. This network is responsible for what we think of as "mental chatter," and is the very activity we want to reduce or suspend when quieting the mind.

The task-positive network, by contrast, represents the regions of the brain engaged and communicating with each other when we're actively involved with a task. The task-positive network includes our brain's *internal* and *external sensors*, the parts of our brain that gather input on what's going on, physically, in our internal and external world.

Some people can switch between their default mode network and their task-positive network very quickly. Based on the research thus far, though, these two networks operate mostly exclusively of each other.[25] Therefore, when we're engaged in a highly demanding task, the mind clears.

Meditations that ask us to repeat a mantra or focus on the world around us through active listening, breath monitoring, or walking can activate our task-positive network.[26] And, some studies on meditation have shown that practitioners can change how these two networks operate, even when they are *not* meditating.[27]

However, for those of us who have a particularly active default mode network, people who have trouble "shutting off" their mind—sometimes the breath is not enough to anchor attention. We need a little extra help.

Luckily, other tasks—especially those that require physical coordination or intense focus—can also serve this function. Perhaps one reason intense physical activity can be so cathartic is because it gets us out of our heads for a while. In my high school gymnastics team, we noticed that we performed our routines using muscle memory, not mental memory. After a slipup, a teammate would often comment, "I started thinking."

We might assume meditation is a mental activity, but it's often the opposite. Meditation brings us *out* of our minds *into* our bodies (physical, energetic, and emotional) in an experience that is mainly sensory in nature. If we're actively attending to our senses, paying attention to the information they bring in, our wandering mind automatically settles.

Many meditation traditions initiate practitioners with some variation of *breath awareness*—a minute-to-learn, lifetime-to-master exercise that

---

[25] *Neural antagonistic mechanism between default-mode and task-positive networks,* Cheng, Yuan, Wang, & Wang, from *Neurocomputing* volume 417. (December 5, 2020)

[26] *Meditation experience is associated with differences in default mode network activity and connectivity,* Brewer, Worhunsky, Gray, Tang, Weber, & Kober (December 13, 2011)

[27] *Tuning out: How brains benefit from meditation,* Yale University, Medical Express (November 11, 2011)

draws our attention to various aspects of the breath. When we're successful with it, our intense focus on the breath can pull us out of our default mode network and into our task-positive network. I love breath meditation, but I only found it several years after I started meditating with my own energy as a focal point. I'm not sure I would have ever developed a meditation practice if I only had the breath to anchor my attention.

Below are three steps that aid in cultivating the technique of quieting the mind and recognizing what a quiet mind feels like so we can more easily "drop in" to that sensation during meditation.

FIND AN ACTIVITY THAT REQUIRES INTENSE FOCUS

Provided we don't live an overly sedentary lifestyle, we can probably think of some activities that require committed concentration. Playing a sport or an instrument, driving in adverse conditions, or cooking are a few examples. Whatever we choose must require our *focused* attention. Trying a new recipe, especially a moderately complex one, might be a great place to start. However, cooking a routine recipe that we could arguably make in our sleep doesn't qualify. *Any activity where we risk going into autopilot is not going to work.*

While engaging in your chosen conscious pursuit, try to catch yourself *not* thinking. Notice when your mind is calm, the way we note the hushed halls of a library when we first walk in or the sudden surprise of silence in a normally boisterous public place. See how long you can stay in that space of just watching the silent mind and observing the sensation of stillness.

NOTICING THE QUIET MIND

Once we've found an activity that clears our minds, we can practice our ability to find that tranquility again. When we catch ourselves in a moment of mental calm, we can immediately pull our attention to our breath and gently bring our presence and awareness to that open, silent space.

Sometimes we might catch ourselves "not thinking" and think, *Oh No! Now I'm noticing I'm not thinking! I'm going to start thinking again.* No need to panic. We can reconnect with our quiet mind by bringing our awareness back to whatever activity had initially engaged our attention.

If we're cooking, for example, we can bring our awareness to the smells around us. We don't have to worry about identifying them or categorizing them—we can just inhale and consciously *smell* them. We can bring our awareness to the temperatures we feel. Are our hands warm? Are our feet cold? We can reengage our task-positive network by focusing on the next step in the recipe, checking on the food, stirring a pot, or actively watching the bubbles rise in a pan of boiling water for a few moments.

Maybe we are engaged in a more active pursuit, like playing a sport. We can expand on a quiet mind during physical activity by bringing our awareness into the body—*physically* feeling the muscles being used. We can observe what our breathing feels like. Is it fast? Halted?

As an alternative way to approach this exercise, we can notice occasions when the mind is quiet as we go about our usual business. We aren't thinking all the time. Be on the lookout for moments of silence in the mind. Even though we aren't actually meditating, we'll be increasing the amount of time, overall, that we spend with an open, peaceful mind, creating space to receive inspiration from the Universe and our Guides.

EXPANDING THE QUIET MIND

Our practice settling the mind apart from meditation helps us recognize what mental tranquility *feels* like. A quiet mind is not a dream we have to chase; it's something we *already* have in our daily lives, that we can expand upon.

After successfully working through the above concepts, we can bridge from noticing moments of silence to sustaining a quiet mind. When you catch yourself in a moment of mental silence, take a conscious breath, focusing on the air entering and leaving your body. Then take another. In noticing our quiet mind and expanding it with attentive breathing, we train ourselves to maintain mental calm, similar to how we might train our body to play a sport.

Sometimes I use a visual aid to engage with my quiet mind. I imagine a point of mist at the center of my mind expanding ever-outward, gently pushing any stray thoughts to the rims. I concentrate on the central point generating the mist rather than on the edges where the thoughts are. Another visual aid for this same concept is imagining water droplets falling periodically into a center of a still pond, the thoughts riding on the ripples to the outer reaches of our consciousness.

To integrate these images with our breath, the drops or expanding mist can be tied to exhalation. Each inhalation draws us to our central focal point. Each exhalation *gently* floats thoughts further and further away. By focusing on the point from which expansion starts, the mind has an image to work with. As the mist or ripples of water expand from the center, the open space in the mind feels larger, more spacious.

When we feel that moment where the thoughts are at their furthest reaches, we can breathe into the space left behind, into that stillness, and it becomes our gateway to deep meditation.

8

INNER SPACE

Developing a Meditation Practice to Support Our Soulwork

Try standing nose-to-nose with a mirror. What can you see? Not very much. We need a little distance from our reflection to see what we look like. The further we step back, the more of ourselves we can view until our whole body is visible.

We tend to live nose-to-nose with our lives. So close, we can't see how all the pieces fit together. Meditation helps us cultivate distance, and with it, perspective. From this slightly removed vantage point, we can see more clearly what we might choose to change, just like having the proper distance from the mirror will show us if our hair is messed up or there's something in our teeth.

Some schools of thought teach that there's only one way to meditate or that their way is best. While we can appreciate their enthusiasm for a method that has worked really well for them or their founders, so many different, practically beneficial meditations exist; I would not wish to narrow your experience to a single type.

I tend to view meditation practice like a box of tools. We might have a hammer in our toolbox. A hammer is a pretty great tool. Even so, we're not going to build very much with *only* a hammer. We also probably need some nails or a screwdriver and some screws. We'll definitely need an Allen wrench if we're going to build anything at all from Ikea.

Hundreds of different types of meditation are out there for us to try, and they all have the capacity to bring powerful change into our lives.

Although in the last chapter I noted that *breath* meditation can sometimes be difficult for beginners, it was the most helpful practice for me in giving birth to both my daughters. And *Lovingkindness* meditation has helped me improve challenging relationships both at work and in my personal life.

While pregnant with my second child, I frequently did a meditation on body sensations and a meditation on emotions sequentially in the same sitting.[28] It was during one of these sessions, as I listened to Joseph Goldstein gently inquire of us listeners, "What is the feeling tone of the mind?" that I realized *I don't feel emotions in my mind—I feel them in my body.* This epiphany completely changed my understanding of emotions. It dawned on me that I experience emotions primarily *as* body sensations.

While it's true that thoughts can trigger our emotions, it's also true that our emotions can cause us to look for ideas that justify or explain them. You are probably familiar with the experience of being "hangry." When we haven't eaten, our blood sugar lowers, we feel surly, and we might start picking fights over small things. When we have the self-awareness to realize that we're actually only *hungry,* we can self-correct and eat something, and our mood improves.

---

[28]   Both can be found in the Sharon Salzberg & Joseph Goldstein course *Insight Meditation.* I believe it is out of active manufacturing, but you can still find it on Amazon.

A transformative example of this happened in my own life with my fear of flying. I developed the fear in my early teenage years. Before a flight, I'd get butterflies in my stomach, feel a bit jittery, and become restless. I *loved* to visit new places, but my flight anxiety sometimes made *getting there* unpleasant.

From various sources over the years, I had heard that the difference between fear and excitement is *breath*. The idea being—when we associate a body sensation with fear, we constrain our breath, and when we experience it as excitement, we breathe freely. As a long-time meditator, I have often navigated fear through breath, so that didn't seem to fit quite right for me—but after hearing this saying a few times, I decided to adopt a playful mindset about my anxiety.

Every time I felt fear before or while flying, I would say to myself, "I'm not afraid; I'm just excited." Thinking this always made me laugh because I sincerely believed I was terrified, but the laughter helped release my tension, and I would feel better.

After playing this Trickster-inspired trick on myself before a flight to California, though, I began to reflect on the difference between fear and excitement as *body sensations*. I asked myself, *Is it really true that I'm afraid? What is this body sensation I'm experiencing?* When I allowed myself to experience the physical feeling, through meditation, *without* associating it to any emotional label, I realized the sensation was far more complex than I was giving it credit for. Yes, there was some fear there, but more prominent were feelings that could be classified as anticipation, nervousness, and, yes, some excitement as well. After objectively assessing these sensations, I realized most of them weren't negative; I'd just given them a negative connotation.

This brings us back to Trickster's role as Guardian of the Boundary and Spiritual Path guide. I had drawn a boundary around my body sensations and labeled them *fear,* and because of that, I *experienced* them as fear. Without knowing it, I had fallen into a trap of my own making, ensnaring myself in the dilemma of wanting to travel but being afraid to fly. Shifting my perspective into exploration and openness allowed me to experience the *same* sensation as excitement and anticipation *instead* of fear, which greatly relieved my flight anxiety.

Regular meditation practice offers us the benefit of distance from ourselves and that distance can help us see how our own thoughts and behaviors trip us up and get in the way of our happiness and success.

In addition to benefitting our Soulwork process, studies are starting to pile up that indicate meditation aids our health and well-being in general. From what has been published thus far, the list of potential health benefits is staggering. For example, meditation can help improve focus, lower blood pressure, rebuild gray matter, manage pain, support weight loss, and even shows promise in the fight against cancer and AIDS.[29]

YES, BUT...

I know many people struggle with meditation. Not only have I heard from others about the numerous barriers to setting up a regular meditation practice, I have experienced them myself.

- I don't have time.
- I don't have a place to meditate.
- I've tried, and it just doesn't work for me.
- I can't shut my mind off.
- I don't know how.

If the Spiritual Path is the road on which we find our Soulwork, then meditation provides the light we need to see the Path clearly, preferable to stumbling over rocks in the dark. Meditation helps us clarify and understand our path more readily. I have seen the *best* results in my own

---

[29] Matthew Thorpe MD, PhD; Rachel Link MS, RD, *12 Science-Based Benefits of Meditation* https://www.healthline.com/nutrition/12-benefits-of-meditation

ELIZABETH RADCLIFFE

life when I meditated three times a day—shorter sessions in the morning and evening and a more extended session over lunch. However, you absolutely don't have to start there. My own practice has varied widely across the last quarter-century, shifting to accommodate my needs. It's your choice how to introduce this practice into your life. On the upside, starting a meditation practice is much like starting an exercise routine. We may suffer from initial inertia, but it's relatively simple to keep going once we build momentum.

Thus, let's address some of those barriers directly.

I DON'T HAVE TIME.

The good news is we can start small. Five decent minutes of meditation a day is far better than nothing at all. Focus on developing a repetitive practice. Even if that routine is about setting aside a few minutes of conscious breathing first thing in the morning or listening to a guided relaxation track before bed, benefits will accrue when we make time for meditative exercises.

We may need to wake up a little earlier or get to bed a little later than the rest of the household to find some time to ourselves. If we have a partner or young children, we may need to negotiate a few minutes to squeeze in a quick meditation. I definitely had to do that when my kids were young, but it was well worth it.

We all have twenty-four-hour days we fill up with activity. If we really can't find the time right now, it might be worth assessing what we spend our time and energy on. Walking the Spiritual Path and developing a Relationship with the Universe doesn't have to consume our lives—it certainly hasn't consumed mine. But it does have to *be* a priority if we want meaningful impact on our existence. It's perfectly reasonable if walking the Spiritual Path is *not* a priority right now, but recognize that as your own choice. We are not powerless in our own lives, though we sometimes resist releasing that limiting belief.

I DON'T HAVE A PLACE TO MEDITATE.

Finding a place to meditate can be difficult when we work outside the home or if our home is a busy place. However, meditation doesn't require a spa-like environment to spend hours in quiet reflection. Finding a spot to be alone five to ten minutes, as close to daily as possible, is plenty as a start and that is not impossible for most of us. When my family of four, with two children under the age of three, cohabited in a small condo, I would sometimes meditate in our master bedroom closet (or even the bathroom). If commotion is a concern, noise-canceling headphones, guided meditation, or gentle music can help.

I'VE TRIED IT, AND IT JUST DOESN'T WORK FOR ME.

Meditation can be intimidating for the beginner, especially when our lives are so full of things to do and think about. Happily, though, the multitude of options that exist means there is something out there for everyone. Trial and error can help us find a meditation technique that is the right fit. If you've had challenges with breath meditation, put it on pause and try a grounding meditation instead. People who struggle to "shut off" their minds might try a highly guided meditation like lovingkindness or chakra-balancing to give the mind something to do during the session. Trouble with visualization? Try a mantra meditation that focuses on sound or a walking meditation that shifts attention to your physical form.

One simple meditative practice I like to do when my mind is particularly turbulent is *counting the breath*. I pick an arbitrary number of breaths— let's say fifty—and set a goal to simply count each inhale and exhale up to the fifty breaths. If my mind wanders and I find myself uncertain which number comes next, I have to start all over again. It's not as simple as it sounds; in moments of acute stress, I have sometimes had to revise my expectations from a target of fifty breaths to being thrilled to make it to twenty-five.

Once we find one or two meditations that work for us, it's easier to get a regular practice off the ground. If home life is hectic and you could use some extra support, try a class. Local park districts, school districts, wellness centers, or continuing education programs often have meditation offerings.

These days virtual classes and apps serve up guided meditations right to our mobile devices. Resources are always available for those who look. Above all, enjoy the experimental element of this discovery period. If something doesn't work, maybe it just isn't what you need right now—keep exploring. You will find a meditative practice that makes your heart and soul sing.

I CAN'T SHUT MY MIND OFF

Although I mention this particular difficulty in the last category, I want to put it under the microscope for a moment. When it comes to starting a meditation practice, I hear this complaint from family and friends again and again. And, while doing a mantra meditation or an active meditation can help, if this is a blocking issue, there might a more fundamental question to explore:

What are you getting out of having a "busy" mind?

Shortly after moving back to Chicago, as my then-husband and I were driving into the city one day, I internally reflected on how *quiet* my mind was. I also recognized just how *often* it was silent. *Wow,* I thought, *I must be the most boring person on the planet. I never think about anything.* This brought on the sudden realization that I had been *getting* something out of my busy mind.

Always having thoughts circulating made me feel more interesting—maybe even smarter. If I was always thinking about something, then I always had something to talk about. If I spent time churning over a problem at work, for example, I had a better chance of solving it, right?

Yet my ability to spot issues and find innovative solutions skyrocketed when no mental noise distracted me from the lightning bolts of inspiration. Insight more easily penetrates a clear mind than a cluttered one, which is why many people find creative solutions while running, after taking a walk to "clear their heads," or during sleep. Having a busy mind had nothing to do with my level of intelligence, and clearing it just meant I wasted a lot less time and energy swirling in internal chatter.

A quiet mind also helps us *listen* to others more actively. If our minds are constantly churning, we're not really paying attention to the verbal input of others, and we might miss something significant.

If you have trouble shutting off your mind, it's worth wondering what you might be getting out of it.

I DON'T KNOW HOW.

Starting a meditation practice can be daunting if we haven't had any exposure to this kind of thing before. Below, I offer a meditative exercise I find particularly enjoyable as a starting point and a list of other potential meditation traditions to try. If none of these work for you, a little exploration will yield dozens, if not hundreds, of meditations to sample.

Try to make meditation a part of your daily routine somehow. It doesn't always have to be the same meditation, the same time of day, or even the same amount of time, but try to put aside at least ten minutes for meditation daily. Like anything, the more we invest in our meditation practice, the more impactful it will be.

Exercise: *One thing that can strongly influence our energy and emotions without us even realizing it is music. Make a playlist of five to six different songs or musical pieces (about fifteen to twenty minutes). If it will be too hard for you to focus while listening to music with lyrics, choose primarily instrumental pieces; movie soundtracks are a great resource for those. Try to pick songs that evoke very different moods; an upbeat piece, a somber piece,*

*a piece that makes you want to dance, if you can find some scary music all
the better (something from the soundtrack for* Halloween, *or* Alien, *or some
other horror movie should work great). String them together in random order.*

- *Find a quiet spot where you won't be disturbed and hit "play" on
  your pre-defined playlist.*
- *As each song/piece plays, pay attention to the sensations that arise
  within your body.*
- *Try to avoid associating any mental images with the music; if a
  mental image arises, take a deep breath and bring your focus back
  into your body.*
- *Where do you feel sensations associated with the music? Along your
  spine? In your chest? Just pay attention.*
- *If a song makes you want to get up and dance, don't. Just* notice *the*
  sensation *of wanting to dance—what does it* feel *like?*
- *Do different sensations arise with different songs? Just notice.*

*This exercise aims to assist us in separating our emotions from our thoughts
and to experience them as body sensations.*

*If you don't already have a meditation practice, try to do this exercise once a
day for a few weeks. If you do have a meditation practice, try this exercise a
few times to see how it feels, then decide whether you want to add it into your
current rotation or not. Feel free to change up the music as often as you like.*

Exercise: *Below, I list several other types of meditation to explore. A quick
internet search or a trip to the library will yield more information about
these and instructions for practicing them. I challenge you to try at least two
meditations from this list over the next month.*

- *Grounding Meditation*
- *Vipassana/Insight Meditation*
- *Lovingkindness Meditation (this is a Vipassana practice, but a spe-
  cial call-out here)*
- *Mantra or Affirmation Meditation*

- *Chakra Meditation*
- *Shamanic Journeying*
- *Walking Meditation/Take a Labyrinth Walk*
- *Heartbeat Meditation (not to be confused with Heart Rhythm Meditation)*
- *Focusing (Eugene Gendlin)*

9

MAKING SENSE OF THE WORLD

Building Energy Sensitivity

Everything in the Universe is made up of energy. That idea isn't meta-physics—it's *grammar school* physics. Light is energy. Matter is energy. Sound is energy. When we talk on the phone, the energy of our voices and words can be transmitted across the globe in mere seconds. When we watch satellite television, the program's energy is transmitted into outer space and then to our living room, bedroom, or wherever we are. Every action we take, every change we make to ourselves or our world, is energy in motion.

Some of this energy, like matter or light, we perceive easily. Some, like ultraviolet light or hypersonic sounds, we don't. The existence of energy is not dependent on our ability to perceive it, nor limited to the scientific tools we have to measure it.

Our own personal energy is part of, and conversant with, all the forms of energy that make up the Universe. Some energetic communication is obvious to our conscious minds. For example, when we sit out in the heat, we *feel* hot, and we may change our clothes or get a cool drink in response. When we hear a loud noise, we may cover our ears. These are energetic interactions we experience on a macro scale. But energetic information is also being exchanged around us, and within us, on a micro-scale, all the time. We are just usually unconscious of it.

It might help to use a wireless network as a model. Our devices access electronic data via wireless networks around us all the time. We are oblivious to this energy exchange, but our phones, computers, televisions, or other devices can translate this unseen information into content we can use.

Imagine if we could tap into and process that information *directly*, with our own minds. Maybe we could, although this wouldn't be as awesome as it sounds. We might not care, for example, that our neighbor is perusing the latest sale on a children's clothing website or that the person sitting next to us on the train is watching an old slasher film. If all the information on the internet came crashing in on us at once, it would be overwhelming—and not very useful.

Wireless network energy is part of the energy that makes up the Universe. But, the energy that makes up the Universe is far broader than that—it is the energy of all people, animals, and things in existence (living or non). We care about this energy and how we interact with it because it's the medium through which we receive guidance in our Relationship with the Universe. We can optimize our ability to collect unseen input by building our energy sensitivity so that we know when to pay attention and to what. One way to begin is by changing the way we look at the world; shifting from a matter-based view of the world to one that looks through the lens of energy.

DEVELOPING AN ENERGY-BASED MINDSET

Physics has taught us that the Universe is made up of energy. What if we started acting that way?

In the same way meditation allows us to take a step back from our lives and ourselves, looking at our world through an energetic lens provides us with a different perspective on problems and potential solutions. Working with energy is not "magic"; it just *seems* magical because we don't have the scientific framework to explain how it works. The energy we are developing sensitivity to and working with on our Spiritual Path follows the same rules of physics as any other type of energy.

When we bring our energy into a situation, whether through our actions, money, voice, vote, or even just *literally* our energy, it's good to be aware of the other energies in play. We start to recognize when the energy in a situation is not flowing freely or where our energy might collide with energy from other sources.

Think of a very controversial issue—something like abortion or gun control, where people who are passionate about the subject tend to fall into one of two camps. Think of all the energy the one group has behind their viewpoint. Now think of all the energy the other group has behind *their* perspective. Those two viewpoints are energetically pushing against each other like rugby players in a scrum. If one group presses really hard in the direction *they* want the energy to go, the other group will escalate and push just as hard in the opposite direction. As long as the energy behind each viewpoint is similar, the issue is unlikely to go anywhere.

These kinds of situations present an "energy quagmire." There are really only two ways a situation like this can move—one side can suddenly get a large enough groundswell of energy to steamroll the other. Or a solution can come from the side, a new technology that renders the original disagreement pointless, for example, and bypass the energy quagmire altogether. In the example of gun control, an innovative technology that renders guns useless (unable to fire) that could be installed in schools, shopping areas, public spaces, or within homes could take some heat out of the gun control debate. (I'm not arguing that such technology exists, just presenting it as an example of a "come from the side" solution). Large groundswells of energy are hard to sustain, though, and circumventing solutions can be hard to find. Energy quagmires are tricky, but we stand a far better chance of getting out of one when we're aware that we're in one in the first place.

To help us evaluate a situation from an energetic perspective, we can ask ourselves:

- *What direction is the energy flowing in? What is it moving toward? What is it moving away from?*
- *Is the energy stuck or blocked in some way? What's the blockage?*
- *Are there other energies around that might influence the energy flow?*
- *Am I witnessing an energy quagmire—a bunch of energy tangled up or pushing from opposing directions?*

Looking at our world through an energetic lens is actually more straightforward than getting lost in the thousands of emotional details that complicate a situation. Like our time and money, our energy is a somewhat finite resource, so we need to be mindful of when, where, and how we spend it. We can train our antennae to hone in on specific circumstances where applying our energy will make a difference.

At work, I can often tell when a minor issue will become a major concern because my energy constantly gathers data on whatever is happening around me. My signals light up when energy is pooling around a particular problem. Or, they may flag when there is a lack of energetic noise; it's *too* quiet. In either case, I know I need to pay more attention.

Earlier in the book, I mentioned leading a stressful project at work. As our implementation date neared, I could tell that the flow of communication was slower than the flow of time; simple exchanges of information were taking more runway than we had. Unless we changed something quickly, we had a high risk of missing our deadline.

I recommended we relocate all essential personnel to a conference room for the remaining six weeks to focus (energy) on the project, reducing the time between communication and action. Typically we would only do a "war room" set up *after* implementation to troubleshoot any issues that arise. The development manager fought me on it, considering it a massive disruption without apparent benefit. I proposed we try anyway; we could always disband if the experiment failed.

The first week he still wasn't sold, but then we really started picking up momentum. We invited our team leads into the room to do a daily update on crucial progress and blockages—we kept all the blockers up on the whiteboard, and we dedicated attention to addressing them. At the end of the project, he thanked me for pushing so hard for that change and credited it as making a meaningful impact on our success. I found out later that he had even written up a nomination for me to win a company award for my contribution. Ultimately, he won that award when *his* boss nominated him for the project's success (among his team leadership over-all). Still, I am honored by how much he valued my partnership.

We have the most significant opportunity for swift movement and impact in areas where there isn't *already* a lot of energy in play. If we jump into a pool and swim from one side to another, we're going to move a lot faster if there aren't dozens of other swimmers intersecting with our path.

Having an expanded awareness of energy is valuable, but it can be frus-trating, too. Not only are we parsing through the energetic input we're receiving and trying to determine how to act on it, but we also need to clearly convey our concerns to others without simply saying, "there's something *here;* I can *feel* it."

On another high-profile project at work, I could tell that our lack of reporting on some minor outstanding software bugs would generate fear among our business stakeholders that we were not sufficiently managing issues. I tried to raise awareness in our technology group of the need to provide more transparency, but I could tell nobody understood my con-cern. To make matters worse, my elevating the risk started causing stress in my relationships with some team members. The program manager I reported to suggested I was being unnecessarily alarmist. So I dropped it. Sure enough, though, a month and a half later, the matter snowballed into a multi-person, multi-day headache to sort out. Looking back, I can think of more explicit ways I could have shared my apprehensions. We learn and improve our skills as we go.

CONNECTING WITH YOUR OWN ENERGY

Below I share a simple exercise for connecting with your own energy based on the one I learned two decades ago. I've encountered it in multiple places since, and it seems to be an effective way to introduce people to this skill.

I recommend practicing this at least once a day for five to eight minutes for two to four weeks. Try to spend time connecting with your energy routinely for the first several months of your journey to build confidence in sensing changes in your energetic field. Consciously connecting with our energy field *attunes* us to the Universe. If we leave a musical instrument alone too long, it can get out of tune. We have to re-tune it. Think of this in the same way. Once you can feel your energy with regularity, modify this as your desire and schedule permit.

Do not get discouraged if you don't feel anything the first handful of times you try this exercise. I have known people who haven't felt anything until the fourth time or even later. Who knows, maybe it will be the first time, or perhaps it won't be until the tenth time. There is nothing to worry about; you have energy and, with practice, you *will* be able to sense it. There is no evaluative measure for how quickly you can feel your energy, but you get an A for effort if you keep trying until you do! Just relax, make sure the spot you use for this exercise is as free from distraction as possible, and don't worry about the timing.

What does it feel like?

You may feel a magnetic force pulling your hands toward each other when they're really close together and/or repelling them as they get further apart. It may feel like pulling taffy, but very subtle. You may have the impression that the air is a bit "thicker" between your palms than outside of them. You may feel your energy for a moment, then have it suddenly disappear. With practice, you'll be able to maintain the sensation for more extended intervals.

Note: You may want to record this exercise using a voice memo on your mobile phone so that you don't have to memorize it. Otherwise, read it through a few times, and then have a go!

Exercise:

- *Ensure you are in a room with relatively low stimulation—lights are low or off, not a lot of sound disturbance, and the chance of interruption is minimal, even from pets. Close doors if necessary.*
- *Set a timer for eight to twelve minutes for this exercise.*
- *Sit or stand in a comfortable position. This exercise can even be done lying down on your back.*
- *Take a few deep breaths to center yourself in your body.*
- *Start by rubbing your palms together vigorously. Focus your attention on the inside of your hands.*
- *Hold your hands in front of you, palms facing each other, bending the elbows at a comfortable angle. Try for roughly six inches in front of your heart.*
  - o *Note: This is only a guideline. Essentially, your hands should be in front of you, facing palm to palm, relatively close to your body, at a comfortable angle you can sustain for a bit.*
  - o *If lying on your back, your arms, up to the elbows, will rest on the bed or floor. Angle your forearms in towards your heart from your sides.*
- *Face your palms toward each other as if you were holding a loaf of bread between your hands.*
- *Slowly move your palms toward each other until they are as close as they can be without physically touching.*

- *Hold them there for a few seconds, paying particular attention to the space in-between your palms. Do not worry if you don't feel anything.*
- *Slowly move your palms apart until they are back in their original position.*
- *Slowly move them together again.*
- *Repeat this process several times, slowly, paying attention to whether you feel any sensation trying to pull your hands back together as you move your palms away from each other or resisting as you bring them back in.*
- *Next, try sliding your palms in opposite directions—toward your body and away—as if you were making a snake out of clay between your hands. (Can you tell I have kids?) Again, no touching.*
- *Repeat this motion several more times, slowly, paying attention to any sensations in your palms or fingers.*
- *After about a dozen repetitions of that motion, try other movements, such as moving one hand upward while the other hand moves downward, or rotate your hands as if they were pedaling a bike. Palms should always be open, facing each other.*
- *Feel free to return to just moving your hands toward and away from each other again, if you wish.*
- *Continue these motions—or others, if the energy moves you to do so—until the timer rings.*

Do not get stuck on this exercise. If it's causing you frustration, keep going through the book and come back to it later. Perhaps this technique is just not the right one for you. The rest of this book does not build on this solitary practice, and if you stay on the lookout, you will eventually find the right fit for developing your energy sensitivity.

If you have prolonged difficulties feeling your energy (more than ten occurrences of giving this exercise concentrated time and effort and still feeling nothing), you may want to journal or draw an answer to one or more of the following questions.

ELIZABETH RADCLIFFE

- *I am having trouble feeling my energy because…(don't analyze, just see what surfaces)*
- *If I could change one thing about this exercise, it would be…*
- *My beliefs about the ability to feel energy are…*
- *I am unable to focus because…*
- *I have a hard time trying this exercise regularly because…*

Study your answers to these questions and see if they offer an opportunity to work on a limiting belief or external constraint that might be getting in your way.

Further Exercises:

If you are comfortable feeling your energy between your palms regularly, try these additional experiments—and whatever other ones you come up with on your own. Continue to broaden your familiarity with your own energy field in whatever way you can.

- *Experiment with different locations around your body.*
    - o *Once you've established a solid energetic connection between your palms, see how far apart you can pull them and still feel the "push" from the energy when you try to bring them back in.*
    - o *Try holding them in different places, like straight above your head, far out in front of you, down low by your abdomen. Palms should always be facing each other.*
    - o *Notice any changes in the energy—stronger, weaker (or easier to lose the connection to it). Also, notice any changes in your body, such as tingling or buzzing, anywhere when you do this exercise.*

- *Can you feel the energy of your chakras?*
    - o *Once you have established a consistent energetic connection between your palms, see what happens when you turn your palms to face inward toward your body over each of your chakras. I find the heart chakra easiest to start with since my hands are already there.*

- o *Move your hands toward and away from your body, and see what that feels like.*
- o *Does the energy strengthen or weaken?*
- o *Is the movement of the energy different? Can you feel any rotation? Which direction?*
- o *Are the energetic sensations stronger or weaker for different chakras?*

- *Can you feel energy on other parts of your body?*
  - o *Once you have established an energetic connection between your palms, stand up (if you are not already standing), making sure to maintain the sensation of the energy or reconnect with it.*
  - o *Gently drop your arms to your sides and see if you can feel the energy between your arms and your torso.*
  - o *Move your arms toward and away from your body, slowly, and see what you feel.*

PRACTICING GOOD ENERGY HYGIENE

Opening ourselves to the energy of the Universe can be life-changing, but it comes with some significant side effects. Unconsciously, we are surrounded by energy all the time. When we open our consciousness to the energy of the Universe, we are intentionally relaxing our energetic boundaries, making ourselves more receptive. As a result, we may unintentionally absorb energy from our environment and those around us. To add to this challenge, we won't always understand why and even *what* we're feeling.

The summer after I turned eighteen, my heart chakra opened up. Unfortunately, at the time, I had no idea what was happening to me. I didn't even know what a chakra was.

When I described the sensations to my English teacher, who had led the Tai Chi class where I first felt my energy the year before, she recommended I check out *Hands of Light* by Barbara Ann Brennan. I found the information within those pages both exciting and deflating. Exciting because the work validated my own experience. Deflating because Brennan's location in New York seemed a world away to a community college student living with her parents in the Chicago suburbs in 1997.

The book explained the chakra system and offered a colorful depiction of their locations in the body. This was my first introduction to them, and, humorously enough, the way the image was drawn led me to believe, for months, that my solar plexus chakra had opened up, not my heart. One day, when I pointed to the location of the sensation on my physical body, a meditation center receptionist insisted that I was talking about my heart chakra. We argued about it in a friendly way, but subsequent research proved her right.

The underlying point, though, is that I had no idea what was happening to me at the time; I felt something strange, and I had to figure out what it might be on my own. These days there are more resources readily available to help us make sense of our energetic experience. Yet, even with the whole internet at our fingertips, much remains to be understood. When strange things happen to us energetically, we want clear explanations and, unfortunately, we won't always find them.

Another byproduct of increasing our energy sensitivity is that we may unconsciously feel other people's emotions. This is not so bad when those emotions are joy, happiness, or love, but it can be unhealthy and unhelpful when they are stress, fear, anxiety, and frustration. Sadly, the latter are found much more frequently in the world. And, conversely, even feeling someone's positive emotions can be problematic if it keeps us hooked into situations that don't make *us* happy.

Around the time my seventeen-year marriage ended, I began to realize just how much of my then-husband's stress I carried around. When he had demanding meetings or rough days, I would experience energetic upset and anxiety sitting at my desk at my much lower-stress job. For many years, I thought something was wrong with *me*. Why did I feel all these roiling emotions when my job and my life, honestly, weren't *that* stressful? Only after he left the marriage and I energetically cleared and disconnected from him did I fully grasp just how much of my energetic experience was tied to his. We have been apart for over two years now (although we still maintain regular contact because of our two wonderful daughters), and, energetically, at least, I feel much more happy and calm since we separated.

I have since come to realize that I feel my oldest daughter's intense emotions as well. Twice, I have experienced an unexplainable depth of sadness at work only to find out later that it was *her* sadness over something that happened at school.

We tend to think any emotions we feel are our own. Thus, when we experience emotions, we may look for reasons to justify them without even realizing it. And if we're looking around for reasons that we might feel sad, angry, irritated, anxious, or depressed, we're likely to find them. As mentioned in the last chapter, many of us have experienced this with low blood sugar from lack of eating. We might initiate arguments or escalate skirmishes over a minor subject when the real issue is our hunger making us aggressive and irritable. If we take on other people's negative emotions, we might create conflict around those feelings when they aren't even ours!

Alternatively, we might absorb the emotions of others, look for explanations, and *not* find them. This may lead us to believe something is wrong with *us*. As a result, we could suffer from anxiety or depression when we're actually enduring someone else's emotional weight. (People suffering from depression and life-hampering anxiety should always seek professional help and avoid self-diagnosing energetic problems.) This can happen when a person close to us is experiencing negative emotions without actually owning them. The whole situation becomes even more confusing if they aren't even willing to acknowledge those feelings to *themselves*. We pick up emotional energy most readily from those we have a strong sentimental connection to. But, we can also absorb the attitudes of random people we sit next to at work, at a restaurant, in the theatre, or on public transportation.

In the winter of 2013, I found myself neck-deep in a soul-shaking Dark Night of the Soul and needed some guidance. I consulted with the leader of a small, local meditation center in the city, hoping he could help. While he finished up some business at the front desk, he asked me to hang out in the waiting area down the hall. The small, cozy room contained a couch opposite the door and three chairs, two of which flanked a corner table. I took the first chair to the left of the door. It was bland and innocuous-looking, the kind you might find in any medical office. However, the second I sat down, I knew something was wrong. Profound sadness and confusion threatened to overtake me. I quickly stood up, frantically brushed off my back, and took the very next seat. Unfortunately, that was no better. The energy felt different but equally destabilizing. I eyed the remaining chair with wariness and hope.

With some resignation, I plopped down in this third seat. What hit me this time was not sadness or fear but raw, energetic power. The emotions weren't as volatile, but the energy was more intense. I couldn't handle it. My gaze fell on the oversized couch. Perhaps if I just perched at the very edge of it, with my back as far away from the upholstery as possible, I could manage to wait patiently in this room without having a total energetic meltdown. I moved and released a sigh of relief. The energy attached to the couch wasn't nothing, but it was manageable.

It's worth noting that I don't usually have this much of a problem sitting down, even at a doctor's office, where you might expect anxiety to be higher than average. The energy attached to these chairs was *way* out of the ordinary. I've never felt anything like it before or since.

We won't always have clarity on what influences our energy field and why. Someone else might have sat in that room and taken no notice of the energy. Or they might have, instead, absorbed the energy as emotions and believed them to be their own. What we *can* do, though, as we increase our energy sensitivity, is practice good energy hygiene to help keep our own field clear. We can also use meditation and mindfulness practices to reveal patterns that may help us, eventually, identify who influences our energy and how.

CLEARING

We take a shower to wash away our physical dirt, but most of us do nothing to cleanse the energetic "dirt" we pick up from our interactions with others and our environment daily. As we work to develop a more conscious relationship with energy, we become much more sensitive, in general, to the energy all around us. Environmentally absorbed energy requires a cleansing practice of its own. Many cleansing practices exist, my personal favorite is *clearing*.

It's essential to start clearing even if you did not sense your own energy in the previous exercise. Physical sensitivity to energy is not necessary for clearing. A need to remove energetic buildup might even be blocking your ability to sense your own energy. Your energy receptors may be numb from managing a constant onslaught of energetic noise in your familiar surroundings.

In the first section of the book, I introduce the concept of Emotional Release, which helps us move *through* our emotions, allowing us to come out the other side with a stronger and more mature heart. Clearing *washes away* the emotion. We use Emotional Release to help traverse our own emotional terrain and clearing to eliminate the energy of others from our field. Unfortunately, from a practical perspective, it's not always easy to tell the difference.

Clearing can give us temporary relief from even our own emotions, which we may desperately need in moments of trauma. Both are excellent tools and, as you walk the path, you will develop the discernment to know when it's appropriate to use which.

There are many different ways to clear—whole books have been written on the subject. I recommend *Clear Home, Clear Heart* by Jean Haner and *Energy Strands* by Denise Linn. Below, I offer a simple clearing exercise inspired by these books that I use to clear my own energy.

It's most helpful to develop a regular clearing practice. If, like me, you live with other people, travel or commute on public transportation, or work in a physical office with fellow coworkers, your clearing needs will be more frequent than someone who lives alone and only comes into contact with others sporadically. We pick up energy from digital communication, too, so be mindful of that even if face-to-face interaction is low.

I suggest purchasing (or making) a pendulum for use when clearing. A pendulum is a weighted object on a string. Pendulums can be obtained from Amazon or a rock shop for $8–$12, so they are relatively inexpensive. At the start of my clearing practice, I used a simple crystal quartz pendulum I picked up at a nearby store. Now I use one made of beechwood. It's lighter and moves more readily, but it cost $30. Think of buying a pendulum like buying a toothbrush or bar of soap. Yes, it may be slightly more expensive than that, but it will also last longer.

Exercise:

1. *Ensure you are in a room with relatively low stimulation. (Lights are low or off, not a lot of sound disturbance, and the chance of interruption is minimal—even from pets. Close doors, if necessary.)*
2. *Sit or stand in a comfortable position.*
3. *Hold the tip of the string for your pendulum between your thumb and forefinger. The pendulum should dangle roughly six inches in front of your heart or solar plexus. No need to get out a ruler—go with whatever feels comfortable.*
4. *Your elbows can be either free-floating or tucked against your side, whichever feels right. (You can also change the position of your elbow during clearing—just know that it will take a few moments for the pendulum's movement to stabilize.)*

5. *Start with an invocation, something like the below, modified based on your own beliefs:*
   o *Guardian Angels, Spirit Guides, my soul, I ask for your help in clearing my energy…*
6. *Typically, a pendulum is held in your left hand. If you are doing so, put your right hand directly below the pendulum. The rotational energy of your palm should cause the pendulum to also rotate. Once you have stimulated this initial energetic connection with the pendulum, you should be able to ask your Guides for help with clearing and experience the pendulum's rotation in response.*
7. *I usually start clearing with what I call "energy detritus"—or the energetic "dirt" we pick up simply by engaging with life among other people.*
8. *As you hold the pendulum, allowing it to swing or be still as the case may be, say out loud your own version of:*
   o *Spirit Guides, Guardian Angels, and my soul, please help me clear all the energy dirt and detritus I have picked up from being around other people.*
9. *Allow the pendulum to swing in a clockwise motion; this signals that the clearing is in process.*
10. *As the pendulum circles, I usually repeat, "Clearing all the energy dirt and detritus I have picked up in my field from being around others" every thirty seconds or so. This is not really necessary but can help us maintain focus on the task at hand.*
11. *Expect each element of clearing to take three to five minutes, maybe a bit more. If this is your first clearing, it may be longer. Be patient and repeat the clearing phrase quietly every thirty seconds or so if it helps you avoid distraction.*
12. *When the clearing is complete, the pendulum movement will change. For me, the clockwise circle becomes a forward and back swing. Your experience may be different, and that's fine.*
13. *Repeat bullet points 8–12 with the following clearing items. Modify these or create your own based on your own needs and experience.*

o *Spirit Guides, Guardian Angels, my soul, please help me clear…*
   ▪ *Any emotions or energy of other people I may be feeling. Return their energy and emotions to them with gratitude for their presence in my life.*
   ▪ *Any fear, anxiety, anger, or distress I may be feeling.*
   ▪ *My energetic cords with others…clear them from past conflict, resentments, and negativity so that the connection between us may be free and open for new, positive interactions.*
   ▪ *Energetic connections to others that are no longer helpful to my soul growth. Disconnect my energy connections with those (feel free to put in personal names here) whose energy is not beneficial to my happiness and personal development, and free me from any energetic bond with them.*

Further Exercises:

Once you feel comfortable with your clearing practice, feel free to try these additional exercises—and whatever other ones you come up with on your own. Journal about anything notable.

- *Clear body part by body part, starting with the head and moving all the way down to the feet.*
- *Clear chakra by chakra, or focus on only one chakra and do a "deep clearing."*
- *Clear your favorite or most used furniture: the bed you sleep in, your desk/office chair, the couch you sit on to watch television, the space in front of the stove or the sink (if you stand there a lot).*
- *Clear physical spaces: your bedroom, the kitchen, office space, and front/entry hall. If energy is stagnating in your front entry, it can slime anyone who walks through the door, including your family and friends).*
- *Clear family and friends, if they are willing (always get permission from someone before working with their energy field).*

10

EVERYTHING IS NOW

A Word on Mindfulness

There's no shortage of resources on mindfulness these days. I practically trip over books, articles, podcasts, and Instagram blurbs on the subject. Thus, instead of delving into this topic in great detail, I will opt for brevity, focusing on how mindfulness connects to what we've covered thus far and how we can use it to support doing our Soulwork.

Mindfulness is the practice of bringing all our attention and awareness into ordinary activities such as eating, walking, conversing, making decisions, cooking, playing sports, and even conflict. Anything that can be done can be done mindfully. Meditation and mindfulness enhance each other. Meditation could be viewed as bringing mindfulness into our most fundamental actions: breathing, sitting, witnessing our internal and external world, visualizing, and vocalizing (as with a mantra).

I took a park district meditation class one summer during my early college years. At the start of the session, the instructor told us, "The only time we can actually enact *change* in our lives is the present." We can't change the past because it's already happened. And we can't change the future because it hasn't happened yet.

"So, if you're not *living* in the present," she asked us, "how are you ever going to change your life?"

Although that statement sounds obvious, this simple question changed the way I approached my life. Instead of daydreaming and planning for the future, I started focusing on the decisions I was making in the moment. Changing my present would ultimately change my future. The tools I was gathering and developing at the time, the ones I share in this book, helped me with this shift.

Quieting the mind, for example, brings us into conscious awareness of the present moment. Meditation helps us develop mindfulness skills at a micro-level by shifting our focus to the subtleties of the breath, external sounds, our heartbeat, and our energy. We can then apply that skill across the rest of our lives. We learn about grammar and syntax in school, for example. Then, we automatically use those skills when we write an email, a report, or a book. In like fashion, when we have an established meditation practice, mindfulness will automatically start seeping into our daily lives.

For the purposes of our Soulwork, a quiet mind, energy sensitivity, and meditation practice help us connect to our inner world so we can listen to our deepest self and experience the subtle energetic shifts within. Mindfulness brings a meditative level of awareness into our everyday life. Then, when the Universe delivers a message, our attention is energetically drawn to it, and our mental space is open and receptive.

Meditation helps us cultivate enough distance from ourselves, too, that we can be mindful of our own reactions to a particular piece of guidance and conscious in deciding what to do about it. We will navigate those concepts in the next part of the book.

Exercise: *The next time you sit down for a meal, or even a snack, try to practice silence. In that silent space, engage your attention in everything about your eating experience: the sight of the food, the smell of the food, the process of cutting and picking up the food with your utensils (or hands), the texture and taste of the food, the process of chewing and swallowing, and what sensations you experience post-swallowing or post-eating. There are dozens of points of awareness even in such a simple task as eating.*

11

FORMULA FOR BLISS

Can We Hack the Transcendent Experience?

The realms of science and spirituality don't always mix well. However, if I've given you the impression that I favor spirituality over science, that's far from the truth. Planning, funding, and executing scientific studies take time, money, and interested people, though, so we don't always have extensive research on every topic we would wish. Some phenomena we may not even know how to measure.

As I have noted throughout the book, my primary motivation to explore spirituality has been experiential. Something happens to me, and I try to understand it. During the initial stages of my mystical experience at age eighteen, I had no context through which to make sense of it. Not only did I have difficulty explaining my internal condition, but even more challenging was understanding *why* it transpired. If we don't understand the cause of an event, we can't replicate it, rendering it a nonstarter in the scientific testing playbook.

Fortunately, studies have been published in the years since my long-ago adventure that might help explain how my mystical bliss came to be and may provide a basic template for how to craft your own transitory transcendence.

It starts with energy sensitivity and meditation, of course. I had been meditating with my own energy for a year prior to any existential escapades. As mentioned in Chapter 8, several studies have come out on the benefits of meditation. Besides the health advantages of meditation, though; some studies indicate it also improves mood, an essential component of mystical bliss.

Not only was I meditating, but I was doing so in direct sunlight, using my lunch hour for reading and meditation outside every day. A hallmark study on seasonal affective disorder (SAD) published in *The Lancet* in 2002[30] reported that reduced sunlight contributes significantly to our winter blues. The research found that sunlight directly affects the serotonin levels, known as the "happy" chemical, in our brains. Not only did I have the mood-enhancement properties of meditation fueling my ecstasy, but sunlight gave me a further blissful boost.

Only recently did the final piece fall into place, though, while chatting with a friend about our differing transcendent adventures, his achieved through psychedelic use and mine without. When the conversation turned to fasting, I had a breakthrough. He commented that what he loved most about fasting was how incredibly clear his mind felt while doing it. I remembered that I had been going through a traumatic breakup at the time of my own mystical experience. When I'm under extreme stress, my appetite disappears. For months I could barely eat, simulating the conditions of fasting.

Recalling that both meditation and psychedelics affect default mode network activity—meditation reducing it and psychedelic use almost shutting it off—I wondered if fasting might have a similar effect. If the

---

[30]   Lambert, Reid, Kaye, Jennings, Esler, *et al.* Effect of sunlight and season on serotonin turnover in the brain. *Lancet* Volume 360, Issue 93480 p1840-1842. (December 7, 2002)

default mode network was a nice-to-have function in the brain, and fasting severely limited the body's fuel, would it stop "feeding" the default mode network, thereby reducing its activity?

A quick internet search revealed a 2018 study of the impact of fasting on internal brain connectivity *did* find hampering effects on the default mode network after fifteen hours of fasting.[31] The study's intent had nothing to do with transcendence and hardly confirms that my heartache-induced fasting contributes to spiritual ecstasy. Still, it opens the door for further research that might prove more conclusive.

It would be interesting to see a report that looks at the cognitive effects of fasting over a month, especially in concert with high exposure to direct sunlight. Maybe scientists could start by looking at the brains of "Breatharians" who claim to live only on sunlight, air, and a little water. Although both common sense and scientific research indicate this lifestyle is both impossible and deadly, one leader of this movement made a thought-provoking comment for why he does it, reporting that he felt "cleaner, sharper...[and] fearless." I can't help but wonder what's going on in this man's brain.

Stepping back from life-threatening cult practices, though, fasting periods or significant diet alteration also play a role in nearly every major religious tradition. It's only speculation, but I'm curious whether religious leaders, too, felt the effects of fasting enhanced spiritual practice.

While I strongly discourage unhealthy dietary techniques, I now believe that a combination of meditation, direct sunlight exposure (wearing proper sunscreen), and a temporarily restricted diet could trigger a mystical experience and is likely what induced my own. Most psychedelic experiences are over in less than an hour. But my transcendent adventure

---

[31] Orfanos, S., Toygar, T., Berthold-Losleben, M. *et al.* Investigating the impact of overnight fasting on intrinsic functional connectivity: a double-blind fMRI study. *Brain Imaging and Behavior* **12**, 1150–1159 (2018). https://doi.org/10.1007/s11682-017-9777-9 (October 25 2017)

carried through an entire year, perhaps because I perpetually re-created the circumstances that triggered my bliss in the first place.

If you're interested in catalyzing your own mystical experience, try taking your meditation or energy-sensitivity practices outside in the sun and consult your doctor about how to practice fasting without compromising your health.

PART 3

I Get By with a Little Help from My Friends

Receiving and Interpreting Guidance

12

HIDDEN MEANING

Finding and Flouting the Trickster Traps of Receiving and Interpreting Guidance

We've already introduced Trickster as a Spiritual Path guide, but he also has a role in helping us navigate the tricky world of receiving and interpreting messages from the Universe—or *guidance.* We even find Trickster in one of our words for interpretation. *Hermeneutics,* defined as "the theory and methodology of interpretation, especially the interpretation of biblical texts, wisdom literature, and philosophical texts,"[32] is derivative of *Hermes,* the Greek Trickster god.

We will always find a little bit of trickiness in interpretation, and interpreting messages from the Universe is no different. Before we can *interpret* guidance, though, we have to allow it within the boundaries of our consciousness—and the act of receiving guidance, itself, is fraught with Trickster traps to beware of.

---

[32] Wikipedia entry on Hermeneutics

The central struggle most of us have in *receiving* guidance is determining whether something is genuinely guidance or "just" our imagination. A more specific way to phrase the challenge is this: *How do we measure the significance of coincidental events?*

Trickster Traps

The Receiving Line

Many of us fall into the trap of setting an extremely high bar for what constitutes a message from the Universe. We might do this by telling ourselves something is guidance:

- Only if there is no other possible explanation for what happened
- Only if we can prove (or believe) it happened *just* for us (i.e., if I weren't around to witness, it *wouldn't* have occurred/existed/etc.)
- Only if other people we share the experience with *also* recognize the significance of the guided moment
- Only if there is something spectacular about the delivery mechanism (a voice calls out from the sky, for example)

We set these high bars because working with guidance from the Universe *is* tricky. Not only do we not want to *look* stupid, we also don't want to *be* stupid—blindly and stubbornly pursuing a particular course in our lives because a hawk circled overhead, or a snake crossed our path, or a random idea occurred to us, and days later we saw a sign on a billboard or found something in a book that aligned perfectly with that random idea.

We set high bars for our own protection. But we risk missing out on potentially life-changing guidance when we set the bar so high that nothing ever meets it.

PROJECTING OUR OWN DESIRES INTO GUIDANCE

Another Trickster trap we fall into is projecting our own desires into guidance. When we're attached (even unconsciously) to a particular outcome or path for ourselves, we tend to look for "signs" we can interpret as guidance that supports the result we wish for and dismiss those that don't align with our desires.

Confirmation bias is a psychological term to describe our brain's tendency to *look* for things that confirm what we want to believe. The existence of confirmation bias sometimes leads people to conclude that *all* guidance is confirmation bias.

This approach is not logically strong, however. Think how dangerous it would be to assume that *all* fevers are attributable to the flu because *some* fevers are caused by the flu. Although a few experiences we wish represent true guidance may ultimately be confirmation bias, that *does not mean* all guided moments are.

Receiving and interpreting guidance on subjects we *really* care about can be laden with uncertainty, especially for beginners and—even after twenty-five years of doing this—for me. Because of that, I've developed my own strategies around receiving guidance. I share them in the next chapter in hopes that they aid you on your own Path.

OVER-AGGRANDIZEMENT OR OVER-DISMISSAL

Perhaps because there is something magical about signs from the Universe, sometimes, when we receive a piece of life-changing guidance, we want to believe it applies to *everyone,* not just us. This is actually a two-sided trap. The first trap we risk falling into is getting so distracted by the power and universality of the message and our role in sharing it with the world that we end up glossing over its very particular meaning for *us.*

I once had lunch with a man who told me he was writing an article about a revelation that came to him. He saw all our negativity, conflict, and bad behavior as human beings as stemming from a deep feeling of being unloved.

Maybe.

I respect the wisdom of that sentiment. But it's *also* possible that epiphany was meant to be something for him, specifically, to explore in his own life—the exposure of a piece of Soulwork for him to dig into and heal.

When we rush to share whatever guidance we've received with the world, if we encounter resistance to our message from others, we risk falling into the second trap: over-dismissal. We either feel confused and resentful as to why no one understands the power of our message, or we worry that, actually, we were wrong all along and this *isn't* a transformative discovery. We decide the guidance isn't all that earth-shattering and we dismiss its importance in our lives.

In both cases, we miss the most fundamental aspect of the guidance: its importance *to us*. Something doesn't have to be life-changing for everyone to be life-changing for us. Guidance that is metamorphic in our own lives is not any *less* valuable than guidance that is life-changing for everyone.

DELUSION

A few times in the book, I've mentioned that one of the most perilous traps of Spiritual Path work is delusion. Joseph Campbell illustrates this in a famous quote:

> "What is the difference between a psychotic or LSD experience and a yogic or a mystical?" he asks.

"The plunges are all into the same deep inward sea; of that, there can be no doubt. The symbolic figures encountered are in many instances identical. But there is an important difference. The difference—to put it sharply—is equivalent simply to that between a diver who can swim and one who cannot. The mystic, endowed with native talents for this sort of thing and following, stage by stage, the instruction of a master, enters the waters and finds he can swim; whereas the schizophrenic—unprepared, unguided, and ungifted—has fallen or has intentionally plunged and is drowning."

He's being a *little* dramatic. And, there is quite a bit of research on hallucinogenic drugs that suggests that they, too, can provide a transcendent mystical experience with the right setting and guidance.[33] Campbell's overall point is correct, though. The unmitigated subconscious can be a dark and treacherous sea. Approaching it through Spiritual Path work does not immunize us from that. For Ron Lafferty, a devout Mormon from Utah, a dogmatic belief that God was communicating directly with him resulted in him brutally murdering his sister-in-law.[34]

Of course, Lafferty's example represents the extreme. Most of us never need fear falling so far into fantasy that we would carry out heinous acts of violence and destruction. Yet all of us wading into our innermost depths have reason to be wary and attentive. All information that comes through our energetic connection is translated by the self into usable material. Within the act of translation and interpretation hides the risk that our subconscious mind silently adds its own spin, or worse, masquerades as guidance from the divine.

Exacerbating the challenge of working with guidance objectively, the field of spiritual development lacks much open-minded scientific study. When

---

[33]   Michael Pollan's book *How to Change Your Mind* is a great resource on this.
[34]   Jon Krakauer, *Under the Banner of Heaven: A Story of Violent Faith* (Anchor, June 8, 2004)

those of us walking the Path encounter destructive influences within the self, we must often navigate the murky waters alone. Obviously, we can (and should, if needed) consult a therapist for help. Still, if that therapist does not understand Soulwork or our Relationship with the Universe, we may feel torn and confused about what is truth in our experience and what is illusion.

How Do We Avoid These Traps?

Take Trickster Traps Seriously

The best way to avoid tumbling into a Trickster trap associated with guidance is by taking the risks seriously. No matter how skeptical we were starting out, we may experience things beyond our ken when we probe our inner abyss. More fearsome beasts lurk in our subconscious than can be found in any zoo. Anger we thought we let go of, desire kept under tight control, and fears we've repressed or talked ourselves out of await their opportunity to surface. Don't recklessly let your ego or rational mind tell you, "I've got this under control" or "I can stop myself before this goes too far." We are often at our most vulnerable when we think we are at our least.

Learn to Be a Bait Thief

In working with guidance, we need to free ourselves from believing the only two options are:

The Universe/God crafted this message especially for me
or
This is all a product of my overactive imagination.

Manifesting our most fulfilling life comes from skillfully navigating the space between those two ideas. Trickster shows us how in a concept Lewis Hyde calls the "bait thief."

According to Hyde, the trickster, Raven, has a penchant for stealing bait off fishermen's hooks when they aren't looking. In doing so, Raven disrupts the traditional rules of the hunter/prey relationship, operating outside of them instead. He eats the bait but avoids the hook.[35]

If we see something we *think* is guidance, but we believe that God or the Universe has concocted this sign *just for us*, we've taken the bait: the meaningful message, but also swallowed the hook that leads to potential delusion.

Although I believe in God, I say my guidance comes from the Universe *because* it places some distance between the guidance and God. As a Catholic schoolgirl, I was taught that God is infallible and not to be questioned. If we believe the signs we receive are instructions straight from God and that our job is to merely carry out orders, it takes ownership of our actions out of our own hands. On top of that, we may fall prey to delusional beliefs about our own importance in "doing God's work" rather than accepting that the Universe provides guidance to us based on our personal Soulwork and the challenges we face individually.

In extreme situations, we may think that we can operate outside the rules laid out at the beginning of this book. That it's okay to hurt others or ourselves because *God* is telling us to do so. The trap of delusion is why Rule #1: *The Universe will never ask you to hurt yourself or another human being,* is the most important rule to remember. Even in our darkest moments, holding fast to this rule helps us avoid potentially dangerous flights of fantasy.

---

[35] Interestingly enough, the fish hook itself is a Trickster trap. Polynesian Trickster Maui's hallmark tool is a magical fishhook. As noted earlier, we often find in working with Trickster on the Spiritual Path that he both lays the trap and reveals the way out.

On the flip side, though, if we're so terrified of the hook that we avoid the bait altogether—we haven't been caught, but we don't get to eat either. We won't fall into the trap of delusion, but we've also missed an opportunity to receive a nourishing message that supports our growth.

Thus, it's best to mimic the "bait thief" in our approach to working with guidance—to take the meat *without* swallowing the hook.

If we receive a meaningful sign that helps us navigate life, we *should* pay attention to it. We can write about it in a journal, engage with the message on a deep level, and keep our eyes out for additional guidance. As long as the message aligns with the rules we laid out initially, we don't need to focus on the loftiness of the source or circumstances of message delivery. If a particular message resonates with our hearts, we should embrace its importance in our lives. How we act on that message is up to us.

SHIFT PERSPECTIVE

Although less alarming and intense than delusion, falling into the Trickster traps of high-bar setting, fear of confirmation bias, and over-aggrandizement or dismissal is unhelpful in working with guidance from the Universe. When our earthbound friends give us advice, how many hoops do we make them jump through to *prove* that they are actually giving us advice? My guess is none.

We may quibble about the *wisdom* of their suggestions, but we don't discount that advice has been given. Imagine the situation from the perspective of the Universe and our Guides, then. They try to provide advice and support, and we flat-out tell them (through our actions, if not our words) that their means of communication simply isn't good enough. If they can't deliver guidance in smoky mirrors or sparkly glitter letters in the sky, what good are they? Seems like that would be discouraging and maybe a little insulting to our Guides.

The most important question to ask ourselves about working with guidance is: *What is our ultimate goal?*

If we're ignoring guidance because of overly stringent "acceptance criteria" or because we believe something only has value if other people validate its worth, we're limiting our own opportunities for growth.

Is our goal to have a joyfully fulfilling Relationship with the Universe and accomplish our Soulwork by walking the Spiritual Path? Or is it to avoid violating a societally programmed rationalist mindset? If the former, we benefit from lowering the bar on our expectations and allowing guidance to come through whatever channel it does.

As part of that perspective shift, it's worth asking ourselves how hard we're fighting to keep our previously constructed view of reality in place and why.

We can be grateful to Trickster for allowing us to see both the traps and the way out of them, but we also need to build a constructive framework for success in working with guidance. The remaining chapters in this section lay out practical strategies to help you develop your own skills of receiving and interpreting messages from the Universe and your Guides.

13

SIGNS, SIGNS, EVERYWHERE SIGNS

A Deep Dive on Receiving Messages from the Universe

One Saturday morning, I meandered through my neighborhood on an early morning walk. My youngest daughter cooed contentedly in her stroller, but my thoughts were submerged in insecurities. I wanted to transition to a career helping people connect to the Universe and find their Spiritual Paths, but what if I couldn't find success on that road? What if I could no longer help support the family, and I trapped my then-husband in a job he found frustrating, stressful, and unfulfilling? Should I quit my lucrative, mainstream career for something as nebulous and marginal as Spiritual Path work?

I am not in the habit of asking for signs, and I'd already received heartening guidance encouraging the pursuit of my goals, but, as I looked up through the vibrant flame of fall color on the trees, I thought, *You know, a sign would be nice.* My heart sinking with the weight of uncertainty, I returned to my walk. Moments later, a young girl walked by. Giant glittering words on her pale pink T-shirt caught the sunlight and sparkled: "GO FOR IT!"

Funnily enough, even with my considerable history working with guidance, I didn't recognize this as a message right away. At first glance, I merely felt an odd curiosity about the shirt. My train of thought went like this: *Is that a Nike shirt? I don't see the Nike brand on it. Oh, wait, no, the Nike saying is "Just Do it." Hmmm...I wonder what kind of shirt that is? "Go For it!" That's an encouraging sentiment. Very appropriate for...Ohhhhh!* Reinforcement showed up a few minutes later in a beautiful hawk circling low overhead. In some traditions, hawks are considered messengers of the divine and remind us of our connection to spirit.

That was a *real* experience, not a dream or visualization. A physical person wearing a physical T-shirt with a relevant phrase followed closely by an intimate sighting of a physical hawk (not a common sight around our area at the time).[36]

I did not take this advice, underlining a critical point about working with guidance on the Spiritual Path. We are the owners of our own journey. We can choose to act on a guided message, or we can choose *not* to act on it. I did not quit my job, and I still haven't, but I appreciated knowing that the Universe supported me in my dreams and aspirations. And I still feel gratitude for that moment of connection and reassurance.

HOW DO WE RECEIVE MESSAGES?

Our first thoughts in wondering how we receive messages from the Universe may default to our dreams, intuition, visiting a psychic (if we are not confident in our intuition), using a Tarot deck, or consulting some other spiritual tool. These options are helpful, but we are not limited to them. We benefit from widening our receiving range to take in messages from anywhere at any time.

---

[36] I had never seen a hawk in my neighborhood before the sighting I mention in the next section. Now, I practically trip over them. It's quite comical. I think there's a hawk's nest very close to my backyard this year because I regularly see them out the window when I work.

The avenues through which guidance comes correspond directly with where we're *open* to receiving it. I typically receive messages through coincidences, music, books, television, outdoor advertising, nature, conversations with other people, and occasionally dreams. For you, it may be different.

We already mentioned attention as one of the tools we would need on our Path. It's the *most* critical tool in receiving guidance. The word *receive* means "to take into one's possession (something offered or delivered)." The Universe may be sending us messages all the time, but if we are too busy worrying over what just happened or what might happen next, we might not be receiving them.

In the first eighteen years of my journey, I never considered nature a medium for receiving guidance. Having lived in urban areas most of my life, my everyday experience of wildlife has been mostly limited to pigeons and squirrels. Thus, I've not really *received* messages through animals, plants, or rocks.

But in 2015, while watching a segment of Sonia Choquette's online *Six-Sensory Training*, Sonia revealed that nature is one of the most common ways messages come through for her. It's not surprising, then, that my interaction with my outdoor environment dramatically increased after that. Now I get messages through hawks, hummingbirds, woodpeckers, cormorants, herons, eagles, and even the occasional fox or coyote. I became receptive in a new way and thus, a new means of communication opened.

Below are some guidelines I follow in determining if a happening is my own projection of meaning based on my hopes and fears or a message from the Universe or my personal Guides.

THE RULE OF THREE

A cardinal way to recognize guidance from the Universe is *repetition* of the same symbol or message, especially a recurrence of three. Seeing a squirrel dash across the road in front of your car? Probably not a message. Having three squirrels fall on your head in the same week? That might be a message.

In the spring of 2016, I worked full-time in a challenging technology career and toiled over a spiritually themed book (not this one) while attempting to give my roles as a then-wife and mother of two young children the highest priorities in my life. Despite my saturated schedule, I felt a sense of urgency around my writing. Sometimes I skipped out on family time or sacrificed self-care just to spend another hour putting words on a page. I wrote on my train commute, over my lunch hour, I devoted whole vacation days to writing and, occasionally, slipped out of bed at three in the morning to scribble something down so I wouldn't forget it.

One sunny afternoon, while my then-husband napped in the other room with our toddler, my older daughter and I played a few rounds of Dixit. A storytelling game, Dixit revolves around the evocative images depicted in a deck of fifty cards. On her turn, my daughter laid down a card picturing a snail. I looked down at the seven cards in my hand, noticing three of my own cards prominently featured snails. *That's odd*, I thought. *This deck has five snail cards, I'm holding three of them, and she just played a fourth. That's a lot of snails!* It seemed like an odd coincidence, but as it could have easily been just that, I put it to the side and moved on without giving the incident much thought.

A few days later, as I played with my youngest daughter on the floor, I noticed one of her animal board books lying open close at hand. The glittery trail of slime beneath the picture of a snail caught my eye. *Hmmm...I* thought, *I never really think of snail slime as "glittery." Also, I never really noticed a snail picture in this book.* I picked up the book and flipped through its pages. *I mean, obviously, this picture had to always have been in here, but why does it seem so....* And then the realization hit. *Oh! Weird. This is another snail.*

At this point, simply because of my history, I suspected my Guides were trying to tell me something. Still, it could have just been that the original snail incident had my subconscious on the lookout for snails. On my high school gymnastics team, we had a saying, "Once is luck, twice is coincidence, three times is skill." When serendipitous events started showing up in my early twenties, I modified that saying as a marker for when I would acknowledge something as more than "just a coincidence."

That weekend, I walked my one-year-old in her stroller around the neighborhood, musing about the snail co-incidents. Deciding to speak directly to my guides, I said aloud (but under my breath—I was in public, after all!), "Okay, I kinda feel like this snail thing might be a message. Send me one more snail sign, and I'll *officially* consider it guidance."

A few minutes after my return home, my four-year-old approached me with two sealed envelopes, "Mom" written across the front in neon pink highlighter. "Mama," she said, "I made these for you at school this week." She handed me an envelope. "Open this one first." I broke the seal and could hardly believe it when I unfolded a picture of a snail. "It's a snail!" she ardently announced. "Yes, I see that." I smiled at her. "It's beautiful."[37]

In my next free moment, I searched the spiritual significance of "snail." The most prominent message, unsurprisingly, was to *slow down*. Instead of rushing my writing, I could be patient with my work and more present in my life. In choosing a snail to carry this message (versus, say, a turtle or sloth, which are also very slow), my Guides also expressed appreciation for my devotion to my Soulwork. The snail's spiral shell symbolizes the journey into the self.

"We see and value this about you," the message communicated, "but it's okay to slow down and be patient with your own progress." Not only did receiving this guidance give me permission to take a deep breath and

---

[37] In case you're wondering, the other sealed envelope featured a picture of a rainbow. Equally loved, equally made from the heart, just obviously not as central to this story.

relax into my writing, but it also allowed me to make more space to enjoy family life and take care of myself.

Some who read this—primarily those who have worked with guidance for years already or who have been professionally trained in intuition—may joke that I shouldn't make my Guides work so hard. I should just get the message the first time. However, I do have a few responses to that note.

I've already written about the dangers of delusion. It can be perilous to project significance into a single event. We risk our subconscious or ego desires having undue influence over which incidents we treat as important if our mind can take any solitary occurrence and infuse it with symbolic meaning. Meanwhile, we might *miss* actual guidance from the Universe because we're giving too much attention to the wrong things. I find it safer to collect multiple data points and notice an overall trend than risk placing outsized importance on an isolated event.

The other answer, which is trickier but equally legitimate, is that the more practice we get at identifying guidance, the better we become at recognizing how it *feels*. The stronger our Relationship with the Universe becomes, the less we need defining criteria to know when our Guides are speaking to us. I lay out several other strategies below, but, especially when first building our Relationship with the Universe and our Guides, the *Rule of Three* is one of the easiest guidelines to use.

SEVERAL SEEMINGLY DIFFERENT EVENTS ALIGN TO A PARTICULAR THEME

The most common experience I have in receiving external guidance from the Universe is when several seemingly unrelated events connect along a particular theme. For example, we might receive one message through nature and another through a book or a billboard.

As I rode the train from downtown to our suburban home one evening, I watched a lecture snippet from Sonia's online *Six Sensory Training* course.

When Sonia shared stories with her students about receiving messages from her guides through nature, I silently reflected that I couldn't remember ever receiving guidance in that way.

The recording concluded as our train neared my stop, and Sonia enjoined her students to "Go out at lunch with the *intention* of receiving a message from nature." Ruefully, I wondered what would happen if I exited the train with that same intention. Ruminating on what the meaning of *squirrel* might be (as it was the only nonhuman animal I was likely to see), I looked out the window as our train slowed on approach to the station. Sitting on the fence that borders the tracks was a large, distinguished-looking hawk. I stared at it, blinking several times in disbelief. And then we rolled past.

My first thought was, "*Whoa, did that just happen?*" This first sighting was the start of a significant relationship I have with hawks. They show up, almost like exclamation points, at key moments on my path.[38]

Voraciously researching the symbolism of *hawk* on my phone during the short walk home, I found that hawks were once considered "messengers of the gods." They remind us to tend to our connection to spirit and can be the herald of meaningful dreams.

I snorted at that. Meaningful dreams were another unlikely occurrence. I have had some incredibly transformative dreams in my life, but never when I thought I *should* have them—certainly never when I *asked* for them. To be fair, I might have been given guidance in dreams when I have requested such help, but I didn't remember anything notable the following morning, nor did I wake feeling sudden clarity on my issue. So, if I was given dream guidance, I wasn't consciously *receiving* it.

That night, however, I had a dream so powerful that I got up to write about it in the middle of the night to ensure I remembered it clearly. In

---

[38]   Trickster fans might note that one of the Polynesian Trickster Maui's forms is a hawk, but I didn't know that until the Disney movie *Moana* came out.

the dream, I met two spirit Guides and Trickster, who nobody else seemed to see. To top it off, it was my first lucid dream ever.

Around that time, I had been listening to a lecture in Sonia's online *Six Sensory* training that focused on intention. *What are your intentions with spirit work?* Sonia asks her students. After seeing the hawk and having that dream, I felt called to help others find and walk their Spiritual Paths.

Truthfully, I'd been drawn to the idea for years, but in a relaxed way, more as a hobby. For the first time, I felt really *called*—like my heart pulled me in a particular direction and not the career path I'd been going down at all.

A few days later, I mulled this over while waiting for documents to finish printing at work. Gazing out the window, I absently watched the boats float by on the Chicago River. A smaller one, a bit apart from the rest, seemed to be calling out to me. One of the people on the boat was literally waving at our windows. Squinting, I realized the boat's name was *Intention*.

I took a picture with my phone because I couldn't believe it. It was as if the Universe was saying to me, *Yes.…You're going in the right direction.… You need to clarify and focus on your intentions related to this work.* So now I had two coincidental events: the hawk, which represented connecting with Spirit, and the boat, reinforcing the importance of focusing on my intentions concerning Spirit work. Less than a week later, a third event joined them.

To set the stage for this third event, we need to travel back two years prior, to early 2013. Struggling with a Dark Night of the Soul on my Path at the time, I booked an appointment with Sonia Choquette for some objective intuitive guidance.

Even though the session did not actually address my current problem, Sonia provided precisely the guidance I needed. Two key themes emerged. The first was that I was a "person of value" (literally the words she used) in the world and that I should not underestimate that. It may sound silly, but I had been feeling so down on myself; her words infused me with the courage to continue engaging with my Path.

The other theme from the reading? My poor receiving skills. Sonia highlighted that, whether it was help, or gifts, or even compliments, I was terrible at gracefully *receiving* from others. That spot-on psychic observation became super obvious the moment I allowed it in. It was, in fact, feedback my then-husband had been trying to give me for years; I just hadn't allowed myself to *receive* it when it came from him. (Poignant moment of marital self-awareness, no?)

Almost two years later, in January of 2015, while on maternity leave for the birth of my youngest daughter, I reflected on that prior reading and decided to actively work on my receiving skills, making this last connecting incident the most meaningful of the three.

Within a few days of the hawk and boat incidents, I visited my favorite tamale food truck over lunch. Even though I frequented their mobile establishment every couple of weeks, I only had very casual, friendly interactions with the man working the window. Embarrassingly, I didn't even know his name. So it surprised me when he handed me a canned soda with my order saying, "Here, this is for you."

I hadn't ordered a soda. I didn't particularly want a soda. I didn't even *drink* soda.

I was confused. Maybe he thought I ordered this? I tried to give it back, explaining. But he only smiled, shook his head, and said with utter conviction, "It's for you."

Okay. Now what? Next I tried to give it away. I offered it to a coworker friend I saw on my way back to work. I offered it to the security guard at the turnstiles. They all refused. Only as I milled about in the elevator lobby waiting for a lift did I *finally* take a good look at the can. At the time, a famous soda company was running a campaign that recommended "sharing" it. This particular can suggested it be "shared" with a "VIP." My heart skipped a beat as I recalled Sonia telling me that I was a person of value.

Here was a gift from the Universe, an actual tangible object, echoing Sonia's words.

Of course, the most humorous part of this message is that the *other* note from Sonia's reading called out my poor receiving skills. I laughed as I realized that I held in my hands an amazing, validating gift from the Universe, and my first response had been to *give it away.* The tamale truck guy said this soda had been meant *for me,* and I hadn't even bothered to look at it before trying to get rid of it. Wow. My receiving skills were terrible. Talk about a hilarious way to make a point.

Taken individually, any one of these events could be easily explained away as coincidence, but when coincidences start piling up, especially ones that resonate so strongly with our Soulwork, it's time to take note.

You've Asked for Guidance

The previous events are examples of guidance from the Universe as advice, support, or encouragement, but not necessarily based on any specific request. However, there are also times when we ask for guidance because we need it (or at least feel that we do).

Sometimes we expect guidance from the Universe to come through in such a magical and unmissable way that we overlook what's right in front of our face, as I nearly did with the soda. But, in other instances, guidance can be so on point that it's practically impossible to avoid the message, no matter how hard we try.

After a year of writing a blog read by almost no one, I felt discouraged and confused about both my writing and my Path. So when Buddhist-based lifestyle company Elephant Journal accepted me as an intern, my heart brimmed with renewed optimism and hope. That summer, I signed up for a booth at the Chicago Body Mind Spirit Expo and happened to be stationed next to Blake Bauer, author of the book *You Were Not Born to Suffer*. We had a great conversation about the path of a beginning author, and when I mentioned my internship, he noted that Elephant Journal had given him his big break. What a coincidence!

He had gotten a lot of visibility showcasing some of his book's initial chapters as blog posts on their site. Maybe this internship was just the opportunity I needed to help me start building toward my dream. I left that expo confident that the stars were aligning to launch me into my new spiritual career.

Fast-forward to me starting the internship and realizing just how much work it was going to be. A high portion of my responsibilities focused on the company's social media presence. As interns, we were responsible for keeping our particular media pages updated with fresh content from dawn till dusk. Even though I could use scheduling tools to automate the timing of delivery, it quickly became apparent that there was no way I could work my full-time job, be a mom and wife, do this internship, and do any other writing at all. Most of my tasks didn't even involve writing. Yet it still seemed like my best shot to build a name on a widely read source, and maybe it would turn into a lead at some point.

What if I gave up my own writing for a while and trimmed a few other areas of my life? Could I make this work? After all, the internship was only a handful of months; at some point, everything would revert to normal, and I could start writing again, right?

Torn and devastated, I asked for guidance. "I don't know what to do," I said out loud to my Guides. "I need advice."

Just then, my youngest child, eighteen months old, walks out of her bedroom with a gray plastic elephant in hand. "Elephant," she says, handing the toy to me and disappearing back into the room. *Okay,* I think, *this seems like something, but what? Does the elephant mean I should stay with the Elephant internship or not?* As I muse over this, she reemerges with a little cloth purse and a plastic toy girl from a building-block set. My daughter is not super verbal at this age, but she manages to make it clear that she wants me to put the Elephant *and* the girl into the bag. I confirm by asking her this, and she nods in assent.

I try.

I try and try and try and try. I can get the girl in the bag with tons of room left over, and I can get the elephant in the bag by itself, but no matter what I do, I can't get *both* the elephant *and* the girl into the bag. My daughter tires of watching this and goes back to playing, but I am still desperately and somewhat violently trying to jam both toys into this bag because by now, I know exactly what is going on. I flip the elephant in all different positions. I try to jam the girl in on the side of the bag after the elephant is in. I even attempt to squeeze the toy girl—as much as you can squeeze hard plastic—into the space between the elephant's legs and *then* squish them both into the bag. Nope.

I sigh. The message is clear. I can only fit the Elephant internship in my life by, basically, giving up everything else, including myself. With a heavy heart, I quit the internship that very same day.

As in the above scenario, sometimes we receive guidance we really don't want and, even when the message is clear, we keep fighting for our desired outcome. Often in cases like this, we already know the answer in our own hearts. We just don't want to acknowledge it. That was certainly the case here. However, it is also an excellent example of receiving unambiguous, relevant guidance just by asking for it.

THE GUIDANCE RELATES DIRECTLY TO A CURRENT SOUL CHALLENGE

As we develop and deepen our Relationship with the Universe and our Guides, we realize how even seemingly mundane events can be powerful learning experiences that accelerate our ability to understand and navigate our soul challenges.

In one of Sonia's *Advanced Teacher* training workshops I attended, I discovered that I had some work to do around jealousy. I have never thought of myself as a particularly jealous person, but I realized that, at the deepest level, I was jealous of my then-husband—and others—for their career achievement.

Although I had achieved success in my own corporate career, I couldn't seem to find it in my writing or my spiritual calling, which left me feeling discouraged and somewhat envious of those who had. I have long believed that someone else's triumph doesn't take anything away from my own worth and value, and I have long practiced balancing joy at another's accomplishment while simultaneously honoring disappointment in my own failure. But, somewhere deep in my soul, tiny green seeds of envy had sprouted.

Disheartened, I went out to lunch. Wending my way through the parking lot to my red Prius, I found, unexpectedly, I couldn't open the door. Was my key not working? I took another look. Oh, wait. No. It wasn't my Prius. I looked around, spotting another red Prius in the next aisle, and trotted over. My heart lurched in horror as I realized the car was parked in a spot for people with disabilities. Had I somehow unconsciously parked there? But a quick glance at the license plate had me audibly sigh in relief—that wasn't my Prius, either.

Finally, slightly exasperated, I spotted my actual car. As I unlocked the driver's side door, I reflected on how all three vehicles had looked exactly the same on the outside. When I looked inside, though, I didn't *want* those other cars; they simply weren't mine. This moment of awareness, brought to me by my Guides, directly linked to the work I needed to do on my own jealousy, helping me understand it at a deeper level. I was concentrating on the success in these other people's lives because I assumed we were the same *except* for the difference in accomplishment—but if I saw their lives from the inside, I wouldn't want to *be* them. I would realize we just have different lives.

A few days later, this shift in perspective bloomed into a further revelation. By focusing only on successful aspects of someone else's life, instead of the whole picture, I was using a scenario *based more in my imagination than reality* to wound myself, to make myself feel inferior or inadequate. Which raised the question, why would I want to do that? How and why I injure myself is something I'm still working through and trying to heal and understand, but the guidance helped bring my awareness to a piece of Soulwork I had been ignoring.

When working on a particular piece of Soulwork, remember that guidance can come in through the most surprising avenues.

Timing

Often, and logically so, timing can indicate whether an occurrence is a coincidence or guidance.

A couple of months after my then-husband moved out, I got two expertly timed messages of support from my Guides over the car stereo. After spending a couple of awkward hours trying to co-host our first child's birthday party post-split, I headed to my then-in-laws condo to witness the opening of presents. Emotionally pummeled, drained, and resentful, I didn't want to spend time around the man I had loved who had left me, even in the interests of comforting my beloved children.

As I started the car, a meditation began playing over the speakers, and I almost switched it off. I never listen to such tracks in the car, and I didn't recognize this meditation as one I had ever heard before. But, realizing that this was probably a moment of guidance and desperately needing the connection and support to help me weather the emotional onslaught, I let it play.

Called, "The Power of Faith," by Gael Chiarella[39] the meditation spoke to the need to reach for something greater than ourselves in our darkest moments.

> "To the alchemist," Chiarella says, "There is a point in [the] process of turning base metal into gold when the earth shakes and the sky rains fire. There is a point when all seems lost. If the alchemist drops the cooking vessel, allowing chaos and smoke to make him afraid, the whole process must begin again, for the alchemist must believe in the process of change. He must, in effect, reach outside himself for something larger, greater, and much broader than his own experience. And as he does this, the shaking slows to a stop, the smoke clears, and the smell of death dissolves. The impurities have been burned away. The process begins its ascent. What was once disaster is now potential gold.
>
> We never know what comes out of the darkness while the whole world shakes. When our vision is choked, and all seems lost. Our task is to reach outside ourselves, to connect with that which is larger, deeper, wider than our own fear. Chaos and outrage fuel movement and movement fuels transformation...."

Listening to this as I drove to my ex-in-laws place felt like a type of grace. I felt witnessed and honored in my emotional state rather than judged. It is essential to connect this track up with a couple of other experiences

---

[39]   *Meditations for Emotional Freedom*, Chiarella, Gael (The Relaxation Company, December 25, 2007)

in my past that give it context and meaning that might not have been as resonant for someone else.

A few years before, I went through a Carl Jung phase. One of my favorite volumes of his work features alchemy. I believe Jung was a thinly veiled mystic who wrote obscurely about his spiritual beliefs to protect his academic reputation.[40] He writes about alchemy in language that aligns with the Spiritual Path and Soulwork. I inferred from his writing that the "gold" the alchemists appeared to be seeking, at least in the Eastern text he focuses on in *Psychology and Alchemy*, was *spiritual* gold—the golden energy of the Universe (you know, the kind that sometimes surrounds deeply spiritual people as a halo) rather than any physical metal.

The meditation track by Chiarella joined together my brief study of alchemy and its pursuit of spiritual gold with the tumultuous emotional roller coaster of the divorce. In my darkest moments, reminding me that if I could just hold on and reach out to the Universe for support, there would eventually *be* another side of this process.

Additionally, meditation experiences from two separate intuition workshops the year before my divorce resonated with this particular track. In the first meditation, I saw a beautiful butterfly, black with iridescent blue markings on its wings, mercilessly ground into dust with the heel of a shoe. There was a moment of utter desolation, a feeling that all was lost, but then a golden butterfly rose up from the ashes, followed by an image

---

[40]   And I now found some evidence that this is, in fact, the case!!!! While reading Stacy Horn's book *Unbelievable* (Thank you Trickster for that find!), I found the following quote from Carl Jung to Dr. J. B. Rhine, leading scientist at the Duke Parapsychology Lab about his research into extra sensory perception (ESP) and life after death. "There are things that are simply incomprehensible to the tough brains of our race and time. One simply risks to be held crazy or insincere. I have found that there are very few people who are interested in such things by healthy motives and fewer still who are able to think about such and similar matters, and so in the course of years I arrived at the conviction that the main difficulty doesn't consist in the question how to tell, but rather in *how to tell it not*." [italics mine]. Stacy Horn, *Unbelievable* (New York: Harper Collins, 2009), 51

of the Big Bang. As if the whole Universe—at least *my* Universe—had been reborn.

In the second meditation, at a workshop six months later, we were guided to imagine a visit to the Akashic records, known as the great spiritual library where our soul records are kept. In my visualization, my then-husband met me on a cliff above the extensive complex where he turned into Raven, the Trickster, and indicated we would need to fly from that point on. I realized gratefully that Freya, the Norse goddess of love and war, had lent me her falcon cloak so that I, too, could fly. We soared to the gates where all the soul books are kept. "I must leave you here," my then-husband said, and I walked in alone. I was met there by Freya herself, who showed me a beautiful phoenix, glittering and gold, rising from the ashes. "This is you." She told me and then delivered a whispered additional piece of guidance in my ear: "Just keep going."

Of course, my marriage hadn't fallen apart at that time, so I had no idea what those messages meant, but I made the connection while listening to the meditation in the car. Even though it felt like all was lost—even though I felt like the alchemist holding on to a scalding pot while my world ended around me—if I could *just keep going*, I could transform into something more than I was before. Like the phoenix, I could rise out of the ashes of my own life.

That was only one track, though. There was still one more to come.

The second one played after I had soldiered through an hour in a room with my ex and his parents watching my daughter open her birthday presents. Since the party was on his weekend with the kids, I left as I came: alone. Even considering the meditation that had played on my way there, I departed a lonely, emotional wreck. But when I turned on the car, my Bluetooth started a completely different track. This time, not a meditation, but an excerpt from a Krishna Das and Sharon Salzberg workshop in

Phoenicia, New York[41] (and I am just now noticing the coincidence of the Phoenix in my meditation and Phoenicia, the location of the workshop).

In the track, a woman from the audience describes a situation that sounded strikingly similar to my own. As I listened to the kindness and compassion of Sharon Salzberg's response, something shifted within me. Salzberg observed that we can be unfair to ourselves with our expectations around what we should and shouldn't feel. She raised awareness of "all the ways we pile on" to whatever painful experience we're going through by judging our own emotions.

"That," she says, "we have tremendous freedom with. We can relinquish some of those add-ons once we see them." When we're already feeling uncomfortable emotions, we don't *also* have to feel bad that we're feeling them. *That*, we can control.

With tearful relief and gratitude to my Guides for picking precisely the right track (*two* tracks!) for me to hear, I decided not to rush to forgiveness. I resolved to stop sacrificing my own emotional state to make life easier for everyone else. Instead, I decided to honor my own grieving and healing. When I healed, forgiveness would come naturally.

Because of the two well-timed tracks my Guides shared with me that day, one of my deepest troughs of despair pivoted to the steepest ascension in my healing process, a stairway to a much happier, healthier future. It would have been easy to just turn the radio off, to dwell in my sorrow and close down. I did not even have to let go, forgive, or "rise above" to experience this transformation—I just had to allow my heart to *listen*. In exchange, I experienced one of the most profound moments of connection with my Guides of my entire journey up to that point.

---

[41] Das, Krishna & Salzberg, Sharon *Live Workshop in Phoenicia, NY (11/16/2013)* Spoken Word 2014

Something Seems "Sticky" or Pulls at Your Attention

Does something keep nagging you? Chances are, there's a reason why.

One telltale sign that my Guides want me to notice something is that my attention will feel drawn to it, even though the reason is unclear.

I've already illustrated this with a couple examples: the T-shirt suggesting I 'Go For It' and the snail picture in my daughter's book. It's as if my heart signals to my brain that something is important, but my mind doesn't know why, so it develops this odd curiosity about it until I understand the meaning. Perhaps curiosity is a signal from our soul that something needs our attention.

Sometimes we don't have time to wait for the mind to figure it out, though, and we just have to choose whether or not to act on the feeling. A few months after my ex and I split, I found myself in the grocery store floral department buying flowers for my eldest daughter's teacher. Because of my environmental allergies, I don't typically buy flowers for myself. Still, I'd heard Sonia suggest buying flowers as an inexpensive, easy way to add beauty to our lives, and some bright orange gerbera daisies had caught my eye.

I kept redirecting my attention, but it would be drawn right back again. I told myself that if I wanted flowers, maybe I should get a bouquet or a bunch of different kinds, but I could feel that I wanted these orange daisies. I reminded myself that I didn't even particularly *like* the color orange, but that had zero effect on my desire. They were only five dollars, and this seemed like a ridiculous amount of internal dialogue over five-dollar daisies, so I bought them.

After getting my groceries home, I looked up the spiritual meaning of gerbera daisies and the color orange. Imagine my surprise in reading on one website that bright orange is considered helpful in recovering from a divorce! (I also read just now as I was re-researching daisies that in Norse mythology, the daisy is Freya's sacred flower. If you remember, she appeared to me in the Akashic record meditation, encouraging me to *just keep going*.) With gratitude toward my Guides and a rueful internal poke for almost *not* buying such a tiny bit of happiness for myself, I put the daisies on the healing altar organically developing on the nightstand next to my bed. Waking up to them every morning ensured my day started with at least a little bit of joy.

Billions of people live on this planet, and while there probably aren't billions of ways for the Universe to grab our attention, there are many different means through which our connection with the Universe can manifest. "Stickiness" may not be the method the Universe uses to signal you. But if you continue to work on quieting the mind, meditation, and building your energy awareness, you will find the sensation that is.

A Particular Path Seems Blocked

Doors are opening and closing around us all the time. Think of the wardrobe in the popular C. S. Lewis book that periodically opened a portal to another world and sometimes remained a plain old closet. Similarly, we occasionally receive guidance that a particular path is closed to us.

It can be hard to accept that a route is unavailable. We may not know immediately whether to fight harder for what we want or to just go another way.

I graduated from college a little lost about my career trajectory. I had majored in philosophy, and the only thing I knew was that I *didn't* want to do that. I found a job working in advertising at a popular Chicago media company, but somewhere along the way, I decided to become a teacher.

For one thing, everyone seemed to be telling me that "I'd make a great teacher." Working my eight-to-five advertising job plus overtime was for the birds—why not get out at three-thirty in the afternoon? Having summers off again sounded wonderful. And I wanted to help the kids, too. How could I "sell out" and work in corporate America? Wasn't being a teacher a more noble and spiritual career?

I'm being overly simplistic here, and hindsight is 20/20. When I initially contemplated this career change, my motivations were much more tangled up, and I didn't really want to acknowledge the less virtuous ones.

A couple other life events moved my then-husband and me first to Indianapolis and then to Austin, Texas. Through it all, my desire to become a teacher remained a steady hum in the background. With some extra work, I got accepted into an accelerated teaching program that held evening and weekend classes and would place me in a school as a pre-teacher for a year. After that internship, I would receive an official teaching certificate.

I *loved* the education classes, eagerly soaking up the information on providing structure in the classroom and clearly defining expectations. Our instructor expertly modeled how to create a fun, engaging, learning-centered environment. Only problem? I couldn't find a job. Of course, it didn't help that I planned to teach English literature instead of math or science—disciplines with greater need. I scored a couple of interviews, but neither worked out. Something felt off. Usually, jobs just fell into my lap; why not now? I began to feel blocked in making this career change, but I forged ahead anyway. Maybe I just needed to work harder for this goal.

Finally, I got an interview for a spot teaching seventh grade at a school thirty miles from my house. Although my preference was to teach high school, this seemed like the closest thing I was likely to find. The interview went well, but the teaching team wanted to see me in action. They asked if I could come back and teach a live class right after Thanksgiving break.

I spent the entire holiday crafting my lesson plan. I consulted with some other teachers I knew and wrote detailed notes for what I wanted to do.

The school had ninety-minute classes, and I had to keep the kids engaged bell-to-bell.

As I drove to what I thought of as my "audition," an ominous feeling overtook me. I felt like I was being prevented from finding a teaching position for some reason and that I would never find a job. I had a quick chat out loud with my Guides. "I suspect that maybe I'm being blocked here," I acknowledged, "but please, please, please, just give me a chance. Let me get this job. I want this so, so badly. I know I can make it work."

I walked out of there with a job offer that day.

At my current corporate position, they had been interviewing candidates to replace someone else. So, when I informed them of my opportunity, they simply decided to hire two people instead of one, and I spent the next two weeks training my replacement. They sent me off with a lot of fanfare. It was great.

In contrast, my first day of teaching was like a bucket of ice water dumped on my daydreams.

I could describe the agonizing details of the experience, but I think it's best summed up by my conversation with a second-year teacher while making copies one morning before school.

> Her: How are things going?
>
> Me: I don't know. It's all so new and emotionally challenging. I'm having trouble sleeping, and I go home and burst into tears every night.
>
> Her: Oh…Yeah, I still do that.
>
> Me: Wait—you still go home and cry *every day*? Why did you come back after your first year?

Her: I just figured that's what teaching is.

Me: <in my head> *What the heck did I get myself into?*

School ended at 4:30 p.m., and I had nearly an hour commute after that. When I got home, I graded papers and crafted lesson plans until midnight and then forced myself to sleep. I woke up every hour and could force myself to stay in bed no later than five a.m. I had no appetite and was on my feet for seven hours each day. Primarily fueling myself with cherry soda, I lost ten pounds in my first week.

On the third day of my second week, as I stood on our front doormat in tears, my then-husband came out to greet me. In the most gentle and compassionate voice, he said, "You know, you *can* quit." Relief flooded in. "Really?" I asked, unable to keep the hope from my voice as I mopped up my eyes with my forearm. It was like he had opened the door of my jail cell. Teaching had been my dream for so long—I had spent so many years and quite a bit of money getting there—quitting hadn't even occurred to me as a possibility until he said the words aloud.

"Even though I wouldn't have a job?" I asked him helplessly.

"We'll make it work," he responded, with no judgment whatsoever.

The following morning I informed the vice principal of my decision. She asked when my final day would be, and I responded, "It would be really great if I could not come back tomorrow." I probably should have felt some shame at the people I was letting down, including myself, but I only felt relief. It was done.

I greeted my new freedom with bright-eyed optimism that slid into dismay as I searched for potential job prospects. An old coworker reached out to see how things were going, and I spilled the whole sorry story. "Well," she responded, "Would you come back? Tim just announced he's moving back to East Texas, and I think his spot is opening up." Tim had worked for the company for close to twenty years. I would have never guessed he planned to leave. My coworker let my boss know I was interested, and after a short conversation, I had my old job back (something I had not even thought was possible since they had already hired my replacement).

I couldn't have had a more powerful reminder of what life is like when we work *with* the Universe instead of against it. If things aren't just falling into place, it's a signal that we're not aligned. My heart knew that something wasn't right, but I begged for a chance anyway, and, as it so often will, especially when we cultivate a great relationship with it, the Universe gave me what I asked for.

From that point on, whenever I prayed or asked for a particular outcome, I would caveat with the words "if this is the right opportunity for me" or something similar.

When I feel as if I can't catch a break with the Universe—the answer is usually not to push harder in the same direction I have been going but to step back and view the situation through a different lens. Often, I find an insecurity or barrier that is causing me to self-sabotage. I hadn't really wanted to teach because it was *my* dream. Deep down, I had wanted to teach because I wanted summers off, I wanted to get out of work earlier in the afternoon, and because other people told me I would be good at it. Part of my Soulwork was facing that harsh truth.

Sometimes on our Spiritual Path, we may have to walk in a direction that seems totally confusing to end up exactly where we want to be. The more we resist that, the longer it takes to get to the life we wish for.

Exercise: *Over the next couple of weeks, pay attention to what's happening around you, and take note of your internal and energetic sensations as you...*

- *Note what's playing on the radio in your car, on your phone, at a restaurant or the grocery store, or in the waiting room.*
- *Note what your eyes fall on when you're not deliberately looking at something.*

- *Note the types of conversations you overhear or things that people say to you.*
- *Note any strange events or unusual experiences with nature.*
- *Note anything that "pulls" at your attention, anything that your mind seems to want to spend more time on.*
- *Log anything noteworthy in your journal and see if you can detect any patterns. Also, even if there aren't any obvious connections the first go-around, don't be surprised if things start happening that link up with what you've already noted. One thing often leads to another in this work. The Universe and our Guides will take whatever opening we give them to get a message through.*

* * *

Thus far, I've focused intentionally on experiences and events where the meaning is relatively easy to discern. This enabled us to focus on the *types* of communication patterns we find when the Universe is trying to tell us something. But sometimes on our Spiritual Path, we experience events or receive guidance where the meaning *isn't* very clear, and we find ourselves needing to wade into the tricky territory of interpretation. We'll cover some strategies for parsing meaning from the murk in the next chapter.

14

ANGELUS AS A SECOND LANGUAGE

What to Do When the Meaning of a Message Isn't So Clear

Learning to interpret messages we receive from the Universe feels a bit like learning a new language, one where sighting a soaring eagle represents encouragement to find victory in our freedom, even if we weren't looking for that freedom initially. A billboard can point us in a direction that has nothing to do with the product being advertised. Or, a chance conversation with a friend can unblock an opportunity for us. We spent the last chapter laying out strategies to build confidence in *receiving* messages from the Universe. But what do we do when the message confounds us?

We want assistance most on the subjects we care about, where emotional stakes are high: romantic relationships, career success, financial stability, our own health and safety, and that of our loved ones. Understandably, these are the areas where we are most likely to be attached to or afraid of particular outcomes. And, unfortunately, that emotional investment makes interpreting guidance from the Universe even more tricky than usual.

Thus, instead of ending this chapter with an exercise, we're going to begin it with one. Start by grabbing some writing materials. If you are using a regular journal for this journey, that would be best, but anything will do in a pinch. Now, take a deep relaxing breath and...*write down everything you* **don't** *want to hear.*

Be kind to yourself and resist the urge to judge what comes up. Just write it down. If you're stuck or confused, I'll offer some of mine as examples. I don't want to hear:

> *that a loved one or I have an untreatable terminal illness; that I'll never find love again; that my marriage falling apart was my fault; that I'm crazy; that no one will ever accept me or love me for who I am; that I'll whittle away hours of my time writing and it will never come to any- thing; that I'm going to lose my job and be unable to cover my expenses or support my children.*

There's more, but you get the idea. You may find some overlap with what I've written, while other pieces won't be relevant at all. The things you don't want to hear will be unique to you and your life circumstances.

When you're done with that, take a few moments to review and absorb everything you've written. If you've really given this exercise a fair shot, some of the items on this list may be deeply personal. If you haven't previously acknowledged them, some emotions may come up in writing them down plainly, offering an opportunity for Emotional Releasing. Honor and be grateful to your soul for allowing these to be seen by your conscious self.

When you've taken the time to process the exercise thus far, take another deep relaxing breath and *write down everything you* **do** *want to hear.*

Try to resist simply writing the opposite of what you *don't* want to hear. Obviously, in some cases, that will be unavoidable, as those ideas are most present in our minds right now—but challenge yourself to move past the work you've already done and allow some purely positive ideas to come through. Here are some of mine:

> *The guy I have a crush on secretly likes me too; I can keep my house without having to sacrifice my quality of life; I'll always have enough money to travel and take my kids to exciting locations; I can find a really fulfilling job and make lots of money doing it; I'll live a long and healthy life; etc.*

Reflect on and absorb what you've written.

Both exercises represent the areas in our lives where we're not neutral. That doesn't mean we won't receive guidance in these areas. We will. However, we'll also experience a more-than-average challenge remaining objective about that guidance.

When we add all our fears, insecurities, and filters into the equation, it becomes highly challenging to process the energetic information we receive without putting an emotion-based interpretation on it. Sarvepalli Radhakrishnan, former president of India, an academic and spiritual philosopher, puts it this way:

> "...there is no such thing as pure experience, raw, and undigested. It is always mixed up with layers of interpretation. The alleged immediate datum is psychologically mediated."[42]

We can tap into the energy of the Universe for information, but once our brain starts processing that energy into thoughts, interpretations and judgments sneak in. The areas where we're not neutral provide information to be aware of as we journey. This is one reason why doing our deep Soulwork is so vital. Without a keen understanding of what's lurking in our own subconscious, it's easy to fall prey to its influence.

---

[42] Sarvepalli Radhakrishnan and Charles A. Moore, *A Sourcebook in Indian Philosophy* (Princeton University Press, 1957), 623

In 2010, Tom Wujec, author of *The Future of Making*, gave an excellent TED Talk on a study he called, "the spaghetti experiment." In the experiment, participants team up and compete to create the tallest structure using only dried spaghetti and marshmallows. The talk is a humorous and highly engaging recap of the findings from this work, and I won't spoil all the fun here. However, one revelation relevant to our discussion is that participants performed *worst* in groups where the stakes were high (a $10,000 reward was offered to the winning team), and experience was low (no one in the group had ever done it before).

Stakes high and experience low? That' beginning Soulwork in a nutshell. We often want and expect so much out of this work and ourselves, especially when we start to invest time and energy into it, that the emotional stakes become incredibly high. Yet, there isn't much societal support or experience to build on, and if *we're* not confident receiving and working with guidance, we can quickly end up in a hot mess of self-defeat.

Our best approach to translating a seemingly ambiguous message from the Universe, then, is to cross-examine our relationship to it with a series of thoughtful questions.

QUESTIONS TO ASK OURSELVES WHEN INTERPRETING GUIDANCE

DOES THIS FIT WITH OTHER GUIDANCE I'VE RECEIVED RECENTLY?

As indicated in the last chapter, we often receive signs in repetition. While the message or meaning of a single incident may be unclear, surrounding circumstances may breathe life into a particular interpretation. With an isolated occurrence, clarity may come with patience; the event may be the first in a series. Even with a solitary episode, if it *feels* like a guided moment, write it down so you can connect with it again later.

DOES THIS INTERPRETATION ALIGN TOO CLOSELY WITH WHAT I DO OR DON'T WANT TO HEAR?

Pay a heightened amount of attention to any translation of guidance that aligns too closely with what you do or don't want to hear. If you receive such guidance, it doesn't mean your understanding is incorrect, but your subconscious might be influencing you. Hold *any* interpretation of guidance, whether it aligns to your wishes or no, in a Tai Chi fist—tight enough to have a hold on it, but not so tightly that you cannot let it go.

When guidance validates our own wishes, we can use *Clearing* to wash away any emotionally influential energy and help ourselves remain objective by asking ourselves these critical questions.

- How attached am I to this interpretation?
- Would I ignore or minimize any opposing guidance?
- How literally am I taking this guidance?
- Is there *another* way to interpret it?

When guidance seems to confirm our worst fears, we can inquire:

- How strong is this message?
- Is this an isolated incident, or have there been other signs with the same theme?
- What can I do, in the real world, to confirm this or allay my concerns?
- Is it possible the strength of my worry is influencing my interpretation of this guidance?
- If it still feels like true guidance, ask the Universe and your Guides how you can mitigate any impact.

Before the birth of my second child, I had far more worries than with the arrival of my first. Writing them down, I reviewed each one and investigated whether I could *learn* something or *do* something to reduce the risk of that concern manifesting into reality. In some cases, expanding my knowledge or taking precautions lessened my anxiety considerably. But sometimes, I just had to pray and accept the fear.

Whenever our emotions risk influencing our ability to objectively consider guidance, Clearing and Emotional Releasing can provide refuge to assess the situation from a more neutral space.

Does this interpretation resonate with my heart? Does it feel true?

Interpretation is an activity of the mind, the center of analysis and rational thinking. Yet, our soul communicates with the Universe through the heart, so we must make the extra effort to *bring* our hearts to the translation table, checking in on whether a particular conclusion *feels* accurate or not.

The meditation and energy sensitivity exercises introduced in part two can help us navigate such situations. They train us to connect with our own energy field, which knows the truth of our hearts regardless of what makes logical sense or what anyone else thinks.

If you're still worried you can't determine if something *feels true*, below I offer a quick exercise to help with that. If you haven't devoted time to the activities in part two—or some other practice like those you already work with—you may have some challenges with this exercise simply because you won't have as much experience tuning in to yourself. But it's worth trying anyway and will hopefully still provide some value (just be compassionate with yourself). This exercise is inspired by one Sonia Choquette teaches in her workshops.

Exercise: *Find a space where you can be alone for ten to fifteen minutes (even if it's only the bathroom, which has sometimes been for me). Take a few centering breaths and bring your focus to your lungs, breathing in and out. Stay in this place as long as it takes to feel present with your breath. When you're there, make a fist with one of your hands and place it over your heart (or you* *can use a palm if you prefer). This helps draw and anchor your consciousness in your heart space.*

Now, say several basic true things about yourself out loud. Pause after each one to assess how your heart feels. Here are some examples:

My name is…

I was born on…

I live at…

My sister/brother/parent is…

Do this until you feel you can discern the sensation of truth in your heart.

Next, say several false things. You might even take the exact phrases you used before and put wrong answers in them. Pause often and allow yourself time to feel. The object is to get a handle on what it feels like to say something that is not true. You might even write all your statements out beforehand so that you're not distracted by "thinking them up" during the exercise.

Once you have a feeling for the sensations of truth and false in your own heart, alternate phrases either regularly or at random so that you can feel the switch from one sensation to the other. Be kind to yourself, relax, and go slow—you might feel the difference right away, or it might take a while for the sensation to settle.

We're not done yet! We haven't covered one of the most common feelings we experience when interpreting guidance—uncertainty. Even our deep self and our Guides don't know everything. When meteorologists predict the path of a hurricane, there are several directions it can go, and each option becomes more or less likely as events unfold. Because our paths are not set in stone, many things may not be certain at the time of asking.

Thus, next, say aloud some things you feel unsure about and see how they feel in your heart. As a compassionate warning, there can be many emotions tied to the unknown. (Does my partner love me? Will I get that job I really want? Will my loved one get well?) My advice would be to pick some ideas with lower emotional stakes, like: "It will be sunny next Friday." Of course, it's perfectly okay to use significant uncertainties; just be aware that the exercise may take on an added emotional dimension in doing so.

Once you have a good handle on these sensations, you can start applying them when interpreting guidance from the Universe or even in daily life when listening to yourself or others speak. Sometimes our understanding of the meaning of an event feels true immediately. But, in other cases, we will arrive at an interpretation that makes perfect logical sense but doesn't actually *feel* correct, leading us to the next question.

DO I NEED MORE TIME AND SPACE TO DECIPHER THIS MESSAGE?

The exhilaration of connecting with the Universe in a guided moment can engender a bit of impatience. YES! The Universe sent us a sign or a message, and we want to know what it means *right now*. However, some guidance only "blooms" at the appropriate time. Sometimes we will not understand the importance of something until later, and while it may seem like a missed opportunity at the time (we all have those in life), the right meaning may reveal itself at the perfect future moment.

Since the start of my relationship with hawks, I've had dozens of significant sightings and many not-that-significant sightings, too. On the other hand, in my four decades of life, I could probably count on one hand the number of times I've seen a hummingbird in the wild.[43] But

---

[43]   Aside from our honeymoon in Costa Rica, which seemed to be infested with hummingbirds. At the beginning of the trip we would exclaim, "Oh my gosh, look at that beautiful hummingbird." And by the end of the trip we were like, "What's that? Oh, just another hummingbird."

in the warmer months of 2015, I had a surprising number of significant hummingbird encounters.

In May, I saw three hummingbirds on a single weekend. Then, on a separate weekend, another tiny bird fluttered before me in Indianapolis. By this point, I was alert to the idea that the hummingbirds could be a sign, but I was still on the fence. All the viewings had been in roughly the same area, and they could all be the same bird.

Additionally, when I researched the symbolism of hummingbirds, I wasn't sure how to apply it to my life. The hummingbird represents joy and lightness of being. Although we can probably all add *more* joy to our lives, I didn't feel like my life was lacking in that particular area.

Maybe it was just an interesting coincidence.

Then I saw another hummingbird in Door County, Wisconsin—a totally different state. As I held my infant daughter up to the big picture window of the vacation condo one morning, a tiny winged creature garbed in iridescent green flew up to the glass. We made eye contact, and it hovered for a few seconds before flying off.

Finally, one weekend in September, I relaxed on a park bench in our suburban downtown area while my youngest daughter slept in her stroller when a pint-sized feathery friend fluttered up to the bushes next to us. It stopped and regarded us briefly and then zipped away.

Three bird sightings, three different states: It was definitely a message, but the interpretation still mystified me.

On the Monday morning train to work, I studied the symbolism for both hawks and hummingbirds again. Not only did I see the hummingbird that weekend, but I had also seen *two* hawks flying together in our neighborhood while out for a walk. At first, they circled high above a house across the street. I wasn't even sure they *were* hawks. As they flew away, I wistfully whispered, "Come back…I want to see you more closely."

Slightly disheartened, I continued my morning meander when, a block further on, the hawks reappeared, flying much lower. One of them glided right above my head, so close I could see the beautiful black markings starkly defined against its white belly feathers. I felt no threat from their presence, but the moment did not feel coincidental.

Maybe I need to investigate this again, I thought. *There's something I'm missing here. I keep having these sightings, but I can't put my finger on what the message is.*

I scrolled through the symbolic meaning of hawks once more, despite having read dozens of versions already. But, this time, I found something new—an article on livescience.com about hawks sometimes protecting the nests of hummingbirds. *Wait, what? I'd never heard that before.* A little train-chair research revealed a study published in September 2015, literally days before my most recent sighting.

Hummingbirds are tiny, defenseless beings. The likelihood that a hummingbird egg in the wild will hatch into an actual hummingbird is an abysmal 6%. Blue jays are one of the most common predators of hummingbird nests, and the report revealed that Hawks typically target mid-size birds like blue jays for food. Thus, a hummingbird egg is almost five times more likely to hatch if there are hawks around. The Article also noted that hawks *will* eat hummingbirds, but only if they're practically starving and don't have heartier prey.[44]

Later that day, I decided to listen to a video from Sonia Choquette's online six-sensory training, chosen at random. Interestingly enough, the first question Sonia asks her class (and therefore me, who is watching) is, *"What is your vision?"*

Hawks soar to great heights. Yet, despite their physical distance from the ground, with their sharp vision, they can hunt for small prey hiding in

---

[44] Stephanie Pappas, *Hummingbirds Use Hawks for Home Security,* 9/24/2015, livescience.com

trees and the underbrush. It shouldn't be surprising, then, that symbolically, one of the spiritual meanings of hawk is about *vision*—balancing a big-picture view of the world with keen sight and clarity of purpose.

As I mentioned earlier, the hummingbird symbolizes joy.

At the time, with everything going on in my life—parenting my two daughters, working full-time, being a supportive and helpful spouse, and writing—I considered letting go of my Spiritual work completely. After all, it consumed copious amounts of time and didn't really seem to be going anywhere. Maybe it was enough for me to focus on my own spirituality and stop trying to put something out into the world.

Hawk arrived as a guide in my life to remind me of my vision to help others connect with their Spiritual Paths—but the hawk and hummingbird encounters *together* synergized into a more comprehensive message. My vision and joy could coexist in beautiful harmony, but if I didn't feed my vision, if I starved it and let it get desperate, it would go after my joy.

The sightings suggested that I couldn't completely neglect my vision even though I had a full plate, or my joy would also start to suffer.[45]

This scenario illustrates how we may sometimes have to sit in uncertainty for a while before the meaning of a message crystallizes for us. Although waiting can be uncomfortable and, occasionally, frustrating, understanding will ultimately unfold if we're open and attentive.

This is also a perfect situation to apply our concept of the "bait thief." It's an interesting coincidence that this study was published in such close proximity to when I'd been experiencing an unusual (for me) number of sightings of *both* birds.

---

[45] Incidentally, the snail message—encouraging me to slow down showed up this same year, giving me some parameters to work with in finding balance in my life; "Go slow, but don't give up / stop."

If I focused on this correlation, I might imagine that this study came out, and these articles were published just for me to see them. However, all the elements at play in the world come together to meet many people's needs and Paths. At the most fundamental level, this discovery had nothing to do with me. However, was there meaning here for me? Yes. Was I guided to have these sightings and see the articles so the message could clarify in my consciousness? Yes. The bait thief takes the food and leaves the hook.

It's only "bait" if you fall for the trick.

15

RECIPROCITY

The Relationship with the Universe Goes Both Ways

Thus far, we've focused on identifying and interpreting messages we *receive* from the Universe—but dialogue is reciprocal. We build our Relationship with the Universe not only in acknowledging advice, but also by taking it seriously and acting on it. When we do this, our actions function as a message *back*—a response. In this repeated process of absorbing guidance, digesting it, and taking action, we find the basic mechanics of a Relationship with the Universe.

That's not to say we should be sitting around waiting for messages. Or that the Universe provides the instructions, and we're responsible for all the action. When we respond to advice from the Universe, the Universe reacts in kind. Sometimes we'll find sudden clarity on our path forward, a new opportunity opens up, or a tangible obstacle disappears. If we continually ignore the signals sent to us, we may get stuck in unhealthy patterns or witness unflattering aspects of ourselves surface in a humbling and uncomfortable way.

As we build trust with the Universe by treating the guidance we receive with respect and gratitude for the connection (even if we don't always follow it), the Universe communicates more and more readily. The Relationship matures, and we trust the Universe to be a significant partner in our lives, especially in those dark moments when we're not sure who else we can rely on.

COMFORTABLE ENOUGH TO DISAGREE

Our Relationship with the Universe strengthens across multiple interactions, and we step, with authority, into our role as co-creator of our own experience. Not only in a "we're in this together" kind of way, but we become comfortable enough in the Relationship to consciously contribute our own viewpoint into our development process, to weigh in on decisions and blockages directly. And, as events in our lives unfold, the ongoing dialogue we have with our Guides becomes deeper and richer, complete with inside jokes and recurrent themes.

In one of the earliest chapters, I mentioned telling my Guides—directly after my then-husband indicated he wanted a divorce—that I was so grateful for their presence, but I needed real, live people to help me heal. In that same tearful conversation, I also kept returning to the question, "Why?"

Why? Why did this happen? Why did they let *this happen? Why didn't they help me save my marriage? Why didn't they work with my then-husband's* Guides *to influence* him *to try to save the marriage?*

The response could only be described as uneasy. As if my Guides weren't really sure if it had been the right thing or not. "I don't know" is how I would translate the response. "It just seemed like you had no space to breathe in this relationship anymore."

I'll be honest—at the time, I was extremely frustrated with that reply. Not only was I heartbroken, but I had two deeply devastated daughters. We would all feel the lasting impact of this change.

As weeks and months passed and I began to accept this new path, I could see the situation more objectively. I acknowledged, begrudgingly, that some good things had come from the divorce, but I was still confused why I didn't get more help *preventing* this drastic, destructive event. Eight months later, in August of 2019, I finally understood.

My oldest daughter has always snored. She was our first, she seemed to be developing fine, and the doctors never seemed concerned about her breathing, so we figured it was normal. When I noticed she suffered from constant congestion in the initial five months of first grade, however, I told my then-husband, "This doesn't *seem* normal." He wasn't worried but suggested I book an appointment with the pediatrician, who took a look and prescribed some antibiotics without any apparent alarm.

A few months after that, my then-husband and I separated. And a few months after *that,* he took our eldest to the orthodontist. He called me after the appointment, noting, "The orthodontist seems to think she has rather large adenoids that might be obstructing her breathing."

I scheduled a session with a specialist, who outlined some options based on our conversation. "25% of the time, this gets better on its own as the child gets older," he said. "The other 75% of the time, kids need treatment, but even the treatment doesn't always work." He recommended putting her on medication based on our discussion. When I seemed hesitant, he proposed a sleep study.

After reviewing the results of that test, the doctor said, "These are pretty bad; your daughter needs surgery." Although the doctor, my then-husband, and my parents insisted on surgery, I felt torn. My daughter had lived with this situation for years already, and it might get better on its own. She wasn't complaining, and the person who had called it out (initially) as requiring investigation was me. Surgery was invasive, removing body parts irreversible, and everything seemed to be happening so fast. After years of having this condition, with no one appearing to think there was a problem, my daughter suddenly required significant medical intervention. *Soon.*

With a few days of reflection, I relented. I wanted my daughter to breathe freely, and this seemed like the best option. I would just have to trust it was the right thing to do.

Thankfully, it was. Post-operation, the doctor informed us that our daughter's airway had been 80% obstructed. Although there were no problems during surgery, my daughter had violent emergence delirium coming out of the anesthesia, prompting the recovery room staff to put her under a second time. When she finally awoke, she was *miserable.* Groggy, angry, refusing to take her medicine or eat anything. She was constantly in a horrible mood. As I sat with her in her hospital room the following day, she tearfully demanded, "Why? Why did you make me get surgery? I was fine. I wasn't having any problems. Now I don't feel well. I'm in pain. Everything tastes bad. *How could you do this to me?*"

Remembering my own reluctance about the surgery, but knowing, now, just how badly her airway had been restricted, I shared my mixed feelings honestly. "I don't know, sweetheart," I answered her. "We don't always know the right thing to do in the moment, but it seemed like you couldn't breathe, and we made the best decision we could because we love you, and we hate to see you struggle."

The moment the words came out of my mouth, everything in the room went still. An arrow of clarity shot straight through my heart. *See?* my Guides told me. *This is how we felt when you asked us about the divorce! We weren't 100% sure what to do, but it seemed like you couldn't breathe in the relationship as it was…so your life went through its own sort of surgery.*

I had enough distance from the event that I could chuckle a little at that joke. In that moment of mutual understanding, I felt closer to my Guides than ever because I could finally empathize with their position.

Our Guides know what we need to work on in life, and they have easy access to more comprehensive energetic information than we do, but they don't know everything. They try to make the best decisions they can about how to help us, at any given moment, based on their own understanding. Isn't that, really, all we can ask of anyone?

Letting Us Learn the "Hard" Way

There are, generally, two ways to learn: the easy way and the hard way. When we see a person slip on an icy, winter morning, and we start to tread more carefully, we've learned the easy way. The person who fell? They learned the hard way.

Our Guides and the Universe can be somewhat protective of us, which sometimes leads them to block a path they think we are not ready for. Sometimes we vehemently disagree with their assessment. In the first year after my separation and divorce, every time I dipped my toe into the dating pool, it was abundantly clear that I, myself, wasn't ready to date. But as the second year dawned, I began to feel antsy.

I doubt I will ever remarry, and I'm not exactly looking for happily ever after. Still, I want to find someone with whom I can talk, have fun, and be physically intimate—a partner with whom I can consciously and mindfully explore what it means to *be* in a romantic relationship. Although I didn't have a hard time finding dates and going out a few times, no one really seemed to fit.

When I sought guidance, regardless of the avenue it came through, the response was always the same: focus on loving yourself *first*. I found this confusing and frustrating. I had already done a lot of work in this area. I thought I *did* love myself. I also felt that I had gone as far as I could on my own. Being in a relationship could help me see my own emotional reactions and behavior more clearly. It's one thing to imagine something. It can be totally different to experience it in real life.

I registered my difference of opinion with my Guides. "I hear you," I told them. "I need to love myself. You don't think I'm ready yet. Got it. But I'm *lonely* for adult companionship. I want to have romantic fun again; I want to experiment with being in a relationship again. *At least let me try.*"

I met someone directly after that exchange in late March of 2020.

Of course, because it was the height of COVID restrictions, I met him online. Although prior experience taught me that multiple drawn-out text exchanges before meeting in person don't lend themselves to dating success, the pandemic made it more challenging to get together right away. We texted for hours every night—about everything. I drew the line at talking on the phone, though. I requested that we meet first, as soon as possible.

As the day of our scheduled meeting drew near, nervousness crept in. I'd had at least a half dozen experiences in the past where I'd built a strong rapport with someone through texting—and sometimes even over the phone—only to meet them in person and *not be interested*. It made for some pretty awkward disentangling. *"I'm sorry. We seemed to really get along, and I liked your pictures, but now that I've actually met you...."* It wasn't even that I found the guys unattractive; I just wasn't attracted *to* them. I needed to feel a spark of excitement, and the text-to-meet formula had provided a low return on investment thus far.

We met in the parking lot of a Starbucks drive-through on a rainy afternoon. Mr. March seemed great. Conversing was easy, and we seemed to have good chemistry. We met up again a few days later for a walk and then started watching a Netflix series together. We liked a lot of the same foods and were compatible in many areas. Everything seemed promising. Only problem? My heart wasn't engaged.

I felt my reluctance to get emotionally closer to him, yet physical intimacy and our time together began to feel hollow without that connection. One night while we snuggled on the couch watching TV, I could feel our hearts talking to each other. "Our hearts are having a conversation," I told him. "It's weird. I've never actually *felt* that before."

He asked me what they were saying. "I don't speak heart language," I evaded. But I did have an idea what the conversation was about. When two people develop a relationship, cords of energy connect them and strengthen over time. I suspected his heart was trying to establish a bond, but my heart refused to allow it.

The dating experience I had before Mr. March went down in flames for the opposite reason—my heart, unexpectedly, got *too* engaged, and I struggled to maintain enough distance for a relationship to develop in a healthy way. I pulled that relationship back to a friendship because I couldn't navigate my own emotions. Clearly, my heart was struggling to find the right emotional balance in relationships. *March and I are just dating*, I told myself. *There's no reason to rush into anything. We can just take it slow and see how things develop.*

A few weeks later, though, we had a minor skirmish, and I used it as an opportunity to exit. My heart showed no interest in getting more involved, and he seemed to want more from me than I was willing to give.

My Guides would probably say they were right—that I wasn't ready for a relationship. Although that's a fair and technically accurate point, I learned so much about my own emotional state from having that experience, arguably far more than I would have learned from *not* having it. I believe that compromise contributed to my growth rather than setting me back, and I think they see that too.

Consciously engaging in our Relationship with the Universe and our Guides benefits all involved. Just like in a physical relationship, partners don't always see eye-to-eye. We have every right to respectfully stand up for our own perspective. When we actively participate in our own learning and healing process, we can find more creative and productive solutions for growth than if we blindly followed divine guidance or if our Guides left everything up to us. A conscious partnership, where we recognize the value of our own contribution and voice, provides the most fertile ground for growth on all sides.

PART 4

The Golden Compass

Navigational Tips for
Exploring the Infinite Self

16

TRAIL MARKERS

Phases of the Spiritual Path

According to my Islamic Mysticism professor, in the Sufi tradition, the Spiritual Path functions more like a map with different places to visit than a single-file trail up a mountain. I love the egalitarian nature of that analogy. One piece of Soulwork is not necessarily more advanced than another; they're just different. We're not all working through the same lessons in the same order; our pieces of Soulwork and when we encounter them on the Path are unique to us. I may sail through Soulwork around gratitude but struggle with self-love. Someone else may have the reverse experience.

That said, the Spiritual Path does have a generic underlying structure that's useful to know as we wade into its nebulous territory. The three main phases of the Path are Initiation, Re-entry, and Spiritual Testing. *Most* people officially start their journey with some version of Initiation, integrate their spiritual and practical experiences during Re-Entry, and then move into the Spiritual Testing phase: where we actively engage with and navigate the Soulwork unique to us. Of course, we can bump into

Soulwork at any point on the Path, but each phase has a fundamentally different focus.

INITIATION

Sudden change, loss, meditation, supernatural encounters, or any experience that shakes the foundations of our reality can deliver us to the doorstep of spirituality. In the *Initiation* phase, we are submerged in the novelty of the spiritual experience, connecting with something larger than the self, expanding our worldview to allow extrasensory input, and noticing how our outer environment mirrors our inner state.

My Initiation phase started with the first time I felt my energy, climaxed a year later in a lengthy mystical experience, and ended with the dawning realization that I would not be raptured right off the planet. (In my defense, amid transcendent bliss, rapture feels like a genuine possibility.)

The banal concerns of the ordinary world fade to the background, overtaken by the magnitude of existence within reach of our consciousness. "Everything is connected" is no longer just a saying, but a feeling as real and intimate as the cool breeze whispering across our skin on a hot summer day.

Every aspect of life takes on heightened meaning as we gain clarity on its role in our soul's growth, whether it's a surprise conversation with a barista or the dynamics of a relationship we've been in for years.

Initiation can last for several months, even years, and converts us from a rigidly rational understanding of existence to one that gleans insight from without and within. Your Initiation may have already happened or may not have happened yet; you know best where you are on your own Path.

Re-Entry

As with everything on Earth, what goes up must come down. The euphoria of spiritual transcendence is no exception. Although connecting with the Universe and our Spiritual Path conveys an impression of wholeness and completion, it's actually a rebirth into a new reality.

When the novelty of our new spiritual orientation starts to become business-as-usual, we have transitioned to the Re-Entry phase. Just like falling in love, during Initiation, everything about our Relationship with the Universe and the Spiritual Path ensconced us in a hazy, languid bliss. But, as strange as it sounds, at some point, our spiritual connection becomes our new normal. Despite how amazing we feel inside, we are not going to ride off into a proverbial sunset. To function in mainstream society, we must integrate our new spiritually realized self with the practicalities of daily life. In our first few years on Earth, we learned to walk, talk, and engage with the world. During Re-Entry, we develop a new orientation toward these same fundamental skills.

I crossed into Re-Entry at more of a crawl than a walk. My transcendent glow started to fade in my junior year of college, so I still had a little immunity from the all-consuming world of work (although I did hold a part-time job through all four of my years at school). In keeping with the journey I had started, I chose to major in philosophy with a smattering of classes in religious studies. Although my more practical-minded parents were chagrined by my choice of study, my courses aligned well with my inner transformation.

In Initiation, we focused internally—on the budding relationship between ourselves and the Universe. During Re-Entry, we shift our attention back to the surrounding world. While in Initiation, we may have noticed where we and those we love are stuck in painful patterns. With our more connected worldview, we had more clarity on the negative influence of these patterns. We may have longed to help "fix" or "heal" these issues for others. As part of the Re-entry phase, we learn that people have to address their own soul challenges. This is *their* Soulwork. The best we can do is support them on their own journey, offer advice if asked, and contribute positive energy and prayer to the situation.

In the United States, many don't find value in activities without apparent economic or leisure benefits. The lofty vantage point of the Initiation phase allowed us to look beyond this restrictive worldview, but we feel the gap acutely during Re-Entry. Operating in a world where every verbal or physical expression of self must be carefully considered for its potential impact on our relationships can be energetically draining, sometimes requiring extra meditation and clearing just to maintain our equilibrium.

During Re-entry, we experiment with how authentic we wish to be about our journey in steering through social, work, and family interactions when others might not be comfortable with our spiritual beliefs.

We will wonder what level of importance to place on surrounding ourselves with those who are also spiritually inclined. Depending on our external environment, they may be easy or hard to find. Of course, there is *no* need to be exclusive in the company we keep. It is always our choice who to be in relationship with and at what level of intimacy. But, throughout Re-entry, we are faced with situations that require us to decide how much of our spiritual experience to share, when, and with whom. This is never an exercise in *right* vs. *wrong,* rather a conscious examination of choices and their impacts.

All the integrative issues mentioned above resurface sporadically throughout our journey. But, we first grapple with the melding of our spiritual existence with our prior and continuing external life in the Re-Entry phase.

SPIRITUAL TESTING

The term "testing" is loaded with negative connotations that suggest the spiritual version is a pass/fail endeavor. It isn't.

Oxford English Dictionary defines a *test* as "a procedure intended to establish the quality, performance, or reliability of something, especially before it is taken into widespread use." Spiritual Testing acts as a marker of our development, challenging us to bring our level of understanding into the world of action. Before moving into a new, more challenging space, we must demonstrate that we've mastered where we are. Rather than lamenting these experiments, we can see in them opportunities to apply what we've learned and grow.

Our Soulwork primarily shows up through Spiritual Testing. At the base of much Soulwork is a wound, fear, or limiting belief that surfaces as resistance to change. Change can be learning something new. Change can be letting go of something unhealthy but familiar. Change can be putting our creativity out into the world. By keeping us stuck, our underlying concern *creates* the conditions for a Spiritual Test. The same way your car getting stuck in the snow creates the conditions for you to figure out how to free it.

As my senior year in college dawned, I still harbored a crush on an ex-boyfriend from high school. Although I had dated several other guys since our breakup, I continued to hope we'd reconcile one day. I knew that mindset prevented me from moving on but wasn't sure what to do about it. Through meditation and intuitive reflection, the solution revealed itself.

I needed to tell him I had cheated on him.

Our relationship had ended two years prior, with some brief contact in between—sometimes initiated by me, sometimes by him. If I exposed my indiscretion, I knew he would never return, slamming an iron door on those hopes. However, if I didn't confess, I might consign my lonely self to a prison of unrealistic reconciliation fantasies.

So, on the next school break, I scheduled some time to see him. We talked about it. He was kind, although probably a bit confused why I felt the need to confess. Since he had been the one to end things a year ago, there wasn't any drama. The whole experience was quite calm and cathartic. I returned to school, relieved to finally release him.

Less than a month later, I met the man with whom I had a loving partnership for nearly twenty years. Closing the door on my past relationship had "unstuck" me and opened space in my life for a new one.

A Spiritual Test can show up in many different ways, but the path through our first one is likely to be self-evident. Some past words or actions, long suppressed, suddenly become unpalatable to carry any longer. Even a few scathing sentiments said in a transitory temper might weigh ever more heavily on our conscience. We may have an uncontrollable urge to apologize, confess, or make amends. If those scornful words were directed at us, maybe we're compelled to confront our tormenter.[46] Whatever we need to do, we'll know it, we'll *feel* it: a drumbeat steadily increasing in volume.

When we successfully navigate a Spiritual Test, the Universe responds. That response could manifest as a new period of connection, wholeness, and mystical bliss. In my experience, though, there is often a tangible result; a career opportunity opens up, I meet a significant new person, I get an unexpected financial increase, something lost returns to me, or I receive a surprise gift.

A pattern emerges as we repeatedly traverse our tests; we have cycles of guidance and learning followed by opportunities for practical application. We find fresh insight through self-exploration and meditation. And then, we must demonstrate our understanding in the material world. Sometimes it is only when we encounter a particular test that a piece of Soulwork, and its role on our path, becomes clear.

---

[46] As always, we should use our good judgment and compassion in any sort of confrontation. Remember Rule #1 and consult a professional before engaging with anyone where there is a risk of harm being perpetrated on either side.

When my former husband left our marriage, he very quickly moved in with his new partner. Our two young girls, one just turning four, met this new addition to their family only a month later. It felt like a lot of change in a short amount of time. As I'm sure is the case with many divorces, it forced me to simultaneously accommodate both my daughters' emotional healing and my own—all while dealing with the complex legal and financial issues a divorce entails.

That summer, my ex and his new partner took their new family to Myrtle Beach on vacation. Rather than mope around while they had family fun without me, I flew to California to heal and visit my sister.

Soaring over the clouds, I let one of my favorite parenting podcasts soothe my nerves: *What Fresh Hell: Laughing in the Face of Motherhood*, from Margaret Ables and Amy Wilson. I absorbed their discussion of how children handle emotional reactions and reflected on how impossible I found it to keep my own cool when talking with my ex, even on routine and necessary subjects.

The podcast helped me appreciate that I couldn't *prevent* my emotional reactions. Instead, I needed to find a better way to recognize and manage the symptoms in the heat of the moment.

During a morning beach meditation a few days later, I noticed a flock of surfers bobbing about in the water. One would attempt to catch a wave, but if their timing was slightly off, the tide rolled over them. Sometimes a surfer would grab a swell only to tumble into the foam a few moments later. And *sometimes,* a wetsuit-clad rider would triumphantly glide to shore. Not only did I realize that surfing was a lot harder than I thought, but I understood immediately that the Universe had provided me with a mental model to aid in traversing those treacherous discussions with my ex.

Instead of drowning in the emotional waves cresting during our calls, I could try to surf them.

As with the surfers, I knew there would be some waves I would miss, some I would catch but then tumble into, and some I would successfully ride to shore. Conversations with my ex would still be difficult. But now that I had a light-hearted strategy for dealing with them, I began to see those calls as an opportunity to practice my new technique instead of an experience to solely dread. To help me remember my plan, I selected the Beach Boys song "Catch a Wave" as the ringtone for my ex.

This learning-application pairing is the primary structure of development on the Path. Sometimes we'll bump into the Soulwork that needs to be addressed first; for example, if an unsuccessful run-in with a Spiritual Test alerts us we have more work to do. Other times, we'll get guidance at the outset and then see the areas of life where we need to employ it.

If guidance reveals that you have Soulwork on setting boundaries with others, for example, or you need to work on saying "no" more often, be assured that ten new projects will soon speed your way, supplying *lots* of occasions to practice saying "no."

This is the cycle it's easiest to get trapped in, though.

If we need to work on setting boundaries, but we don't actually *do* it, responsibilities will just keep piling up until we're overworked and burned out. We might change jobs to escape the situation only to find that, after a brief reprieve, the same thing happens at our new job! This is because the source of the difficulty lies within us, influencing the behavior that creates our challenging conditions.

While embroiled in a particularly tricky Spiritual Test, we might feel disheartened at our inability to sail through with ease. It's in these moments of disappointment, we risk turning away from our Relationship with the Universe out of shame. Unknowingly, we're teetering toward a Dark Night of the Soul.

THE DARK NIGHT OF THE SOUL

I have heard the term "Dark Night of the Soul" used to refer to a deeply troubling time in one's life, something that shakes us to the very core of our being. While I would *never* minimize such life events in any way, I use this term somewhat differently. I believe we can only experience a true Dark Night of the Soul after we have actually "met" our soul—after we've started walking our Spiritual Path, developing a Relationship with the Universe, and engaging with our Soulwork.

The demise of my twenty-year romantic relationship was, thus far, the *most* devastating event of my life, a death of the existence I had known and the destruction of my many happy imaginings for the future. But it was *not* a Dark Night of the Soul. My Relationship with the Universe nursed me through that wreckage.

The Universe never abandons us. In a Dark Night of the Soul, it is *we* who turn away.

Once we've moved beyond the euphoria of connection that comes with Initiation, following the integration of our spiritual self with our physical life during Re-Entry, and in the wake of successfully navigating a few Spiritual Tests, we can feel like we've got this Spiritual Path thing down.

Enter the Dark Night of the Soul.

Our successful experience has primed us for a Spiritual Test where the path is so unclear, the challenge so close to our hearts, that we arrive at a powerful conclusion: even carrying such formidable tools as our deep connection to the Universe, our previous Soulwork experience, and our understanding of our own soul is *not always enough*.

In those moments, we can't fathom what *more* we could bring to the table. It seems hopeless. We feel like a failure and begin to turn away from our connection in shame and confusion. We question whether we knew what we were doing at all. Is there really such a thing as the Spiritual Path? Do we really have a Relationship with the Universe? Was this all just a delusional dream? Why aren't our former tools working? Facing a colossal crisis of faith, the material world serenades us with a siren song of safety—and we surrender.

A few years after my then-husband and I moved back to Chicago, I developed an odd curiosity about a male coworker that disrupted my life. He was constantly on my mind, yet I could barely remember what he looked like. His presence had lodged itself in my being without me having any conscious input on the matter.

Even though we worked together, I only saw him periodically at first. Our interactions were nothing special. In fact, I was pretty sure he *didn't* think much of me. He was resistant to my ideas, and our early work chats were often contentious. Somehow, though, my unwelcome fixation persisted.

One January morning, I heard him talking to a female coworker in the cubicle next door. Irrationally jealous, I wondered if he would stop by my cube and say hi afterward. *Probably not*, I thought, then furiously chastised myself for caring. I believed myself to be in a loving, happy marriage. I had been with my then-husband for nearly eleven years. Together we'd weathered many ups and downs and were looking forward to building a family together, something I wanted more than anything.

What was WRONG with me?

But he did end up stopping by, and as he stepped into my cube and started talking, our eyes locked together. His voice fell away and we stared at each other in silence. I don't know what he saw in my eyes that day: probably a depth of feeling he wasn't expecting. It stopped him in his tracks.

So began my slow, tumultuous slide into an extramarital affair.

I loved my then-husband and had no intention of dishonoring our union. I wondered how I could have such intense feelings for someone else.

Most disorienting was the overwhelming guilt. Not when I gave in to the temptation to spend time with my coworker, but when I resisted. Although the affair was never physically consummated, I felt more guilty denying my coworker time and attention than I did for giving it to someone other than my husband. It didn't make any sense! How could that be? I actively combatted my feelings. Though I never wished to be with my coworker at night when I was with my family, my attention revolved around him at work.

I confessed the situation to my then-husband early on. Even then, I knew I secretly hoped that exposing myself would give me the strength to put an end to it. I didn't want to betray my marriage. I didn't want to hurt anybody. Yet here I was, doing just that.

Furious and hurt, my then-husband forbade me to see my coworker. I tried. We managed to separate from each other for about a week. My coworker looked harried, and I felt the same. We were both suffering. It was nearly impossible to avoid regular contact as we worked closely together on a small team. In retrospect, perhaps quitting my job would have been best. Apart from my relationship situation, though, I was so happy at work, I couldn't bear the thought of leaving.

In disgrace, I sought solace and answers in meditation. When that didn't work, I turned away from it entirely. How could I connect with the Universe while engaging in such deceptive and unhealthy behavior? I felt unworthy of my relationship with my then-husband and unworthy of my Relationship with the Universe.

I was lost in a Dark Night of the Soul.

After months of fighting this on-again, off-again affair, I decided to see a past-life regressionist. I had previously had a life-changing regression session and wondered if another could shed light on my difficulty letting this go.

Under hypnosis, I watched my coworker and I grow up as childhood friends in a tiny rural hamlet. As we aged, friendship matured into love. I saw myself beaming with shy joy in a simple country dress, a crown of flowers in my long blond hair for our modest rural wedding. Something happened a handful of years later, though, that I would not let myself see. My regression exploration met with a cold wall of blackness coupled with intense guilt. My soul was curled up, rocking herself, in a dark and empty void. (I later pieced together that I might have committed suicide, although I'm still unsure what I bumped into in my psyche.) Speaking as myself in that life, I cried that I was so sorry for what I had done to him and our family and that I missed him so much. Loneliness engulfed me in that bleak place.

The last time I sought answers through past-life regression, my feelings were immediately "cured" when it concluded. Unfortunately, this time I wasn't so lucky. But the history gave me much to mull over in trying to find my way out of the Dark Night.

Having struggled with this dilemma for almost three years, relief washed over me when, a few months after my regression appointment, the solution slowly emerged. I needed to forgive myself for whatever I had done in that past life. No doubt it had been a terrible thing. No doubt it had a profound emotional impact on both of us that carried into this lifetime. But it had happened long ago, in a previous incarnation. I couldn't change the past. Allowing *that* past to wreak havoc on *this* present helped no one. I performed a simple releasing ritual while in the Mother's room at work. I forgave myself and asked my Guides for help freeing the current situation from past emotions. Finally liberated, I could move beyond the intensity of that ill-fated attraction into a much healthier place.

Do I wish I had handled that situation better? Yes. Do I wish I had never cheated on my then-husband at all? Yes. However, it felt like a tiny victory to claw my way back to balance after years of torment. As I started timidly, tentatively, re-engaging my connection to the Universe, I found no censure, only love. The Universe knows our hearts, and my heart had always been trying to navigate the situation from a place of love and compassion for everyone involved, as lost as I sometimes felt.

Although it's embarrassing and doesn't reflect well on my character, I share this story because a Dark Night of the Soul can catch us off guard, even after years of doing spiritual work. We may find ourselves suddenly swirling in doubt, just weeks after bliss, completely confused by the difference. We become uncomfortable with our connection to the Universe because we're uncomfortable with our own limitations. A Dark Night of the Soul can reveal that we're not as strong as we thought, or as kind, or as wise, or as loving, or some other trait we were at home with. Even with a full spiritual arsenal at hand, we, too, can fall prey to a trial that strikes our very core.

We don't *have* to experience a Dark Night of the Soul. I've managed to narrowly avoid two while floundering in my book writing and recovering from my divorce. Perhaps I have finally learned how to recognize the warning signs from the three I've already been through. Fear and shame are the most common entry points, but any negative emotion that inhibits our Relationship with the Universe can drag us down. When we feel ourselves succumbing to negative emotions, we can remember that our Guides are always in our corner when we're working on our soul growth. The line we keep open with the Universe will eventually be the rope we climb out of the dark.

17

FOOL'S GOLD

The Art of Finding

In the early days of walking my Spiritual Path, I loved to visit the library. I would walk up and down the nonfiction aisles with my eyes half-closed, allowing my energy to draw me to a book. If someone approached, I would quickly act engrossed with whatever subject area happened to be in front of me. When they departed, I resumed my energetic exploration.

I found many pivotal books on my Path through this process. It's how I found Joseph Campbell's *Hero with a Thousand Faces* and his VHS lectures that catalyzed my transcendent experience. It's how I found Idries Shah's book, *The Sufis*, which introduced me to the concept of mysticism. It's how I found Sonia Choquette's book *Diary of a Psychic,* which eventually led me to train with Sonia on honing my intuition and connecting with my personal guides. And it's how I found Trickster.

The memory still makes me chuckle. My energy led me precisely to the spine of *Trickster Makes This World* by Lewis Hyde, but I was *so* disappointed. This couldn't be the book I was meant to read. It looked nothing like I expected the next book on my path to look. It wasn't about anything that seemed spiritual, or relevant to my Path, or frankly, even…*interesting*. (No offense intended, Professor Hyde).

I actually put it back on the shelf.

Physically tracing my fingers over the other volumes in the bookcase, I hoped to feel an energetic tingle for one of the more promising-looking titles nearby. Nope. Sighing, I pulled Trickster back out—this was the book I was meant to find. I checked it out of the library and have never been the same since.

At the time, I didn't realize that I had been using a type of skill in these library missions: a gift from Trickster, the *Art of Finding*.

Think of all the time we spend looking for things: keys, wallets, jobs, our life partner, our life *purpose*. What if we could just locate what we need *without* looking for it? How much more could we do if we didn't fill so much space with *looking*? Not only is the *Art of Finding* a life-changing skill for commonplace concerns, but we often discover our Soulwork leveraging this same skill. And, it's frequently how we find strategies to aid in working through the challenges of our souls.

Unlike co-creation, which primarily requires alignment to activate in our lives, *finding* requires total trust. To *find,* we must move our conscious minds *completely* out of the way, a none-too-easy task. In other words, to practice finding, we have to stop looking.

What is the difference between *looking* and *finding*?

Both finding and looking start with a need or desire, such as, *"I need to find my keys."* Typically, the way we have been trained to *look*, we would start with a list of mental questions: *Where did I last see them? When did I last use them? Has anyone else around here seen them?* We rummage through our brain for memories so we can rummage through our environment for the keys.

We might find the keys quickly. We might not.

How does this work in the Art of Finding? First, I ask my Guides (and sometimes Trickster directly), *"Can you please help me find my keys?"* Then I quiet my mind and turn my attention inward. I keep my eyes at least partially open. I want to avoid visual distraction, but I'd also like to avoid bumping into things. Turning up my energetic awareness, I try to sense where I should walk, what I should open, pick up, or look under.

When I can do this successfully, I locate whatever I need in a fraction of the time it would have taken me to *look*. This conclusion is based on retrieving several items (belts, wallets, keys, clothes, books) from places where I would only have thought to look maybe fourth or fifth in sequence, if at all. In one humorous incident, while *finding* a belt, I immediately walked over to a large pile of my then-husband's sweaters, scooped my arm underneath, and picked them all up. There lay the belt, previously hidden from view. I doubt I would have even *thought* to look there.

It sounds simple, and, in a way, it *is*. We don't actually have to do very much—or, at least, our brains don't. On the other hand, it's harder to keep our "thinking selves" out of the way than it seems—even for experienced meditators and energy workers.

For example, if we're trying to *find* car keys and have a mental picture of the last place we saw them, we probably can't *find* them anymore—at least, not until we check that location. A thought, an image, or even a subtle feeling of where the keys must be can interfere with the openness required for *finding*.

Finding can be challenging when others are around, as well. Self-consciousness distracts us. *Do I look silly? What if I can't do it?* Suddenly, we're not *finding* anymore; we're *performing*. Perhaps we're even trying to *prove* we can do it. All of that gets in the way of simply doing it—stakes high, experience low; not a recipe for success at anything.

Our rational mind is so used to being in control that when we're trying to *find* a specific article, like our wallet, the logical part of our brains follows us around like a child banging a pot and yelling in protest. Our minds are frustrated we're not doing things the way we always do. *Aren't we just wasting time?* Our minds inquire. *Shouldn't we take a more rational approach? Maybe we should be listing possible locations where the wallet could be? Or asking if anyone has seen it? Or checking the last place we remember seeing it? Seriously? This is what we're doing? Walking around aimlessly?*

One afternoon, as my then-husband bathed our infant daughter, he asked me to bring him the bath crayons we had just bought. Since I didn't know where they were, I decided to try to *find* them. Half-closing my eyes, I let my energetic awareness take over and walked directly into our second bedroom and stood in front of the bed.

Opening my eyes fully, I scanned the rumple of blankets but didn't see them. Doubt crept in. *Why on Earth would they be in the bedroom?* Maybe I was doing something wrong. Then a memory snapped into focus. I had last seen them on the kitchen counter—surely, they were still on the counter. Of course, now I can no longer *find* the crayons because I can't escape the idea that they must be on the counter. So, I start *looking*. I go over to the bar and sift through papers, lifting up objects and peering underneath.

My then-husband comes out to see what's taking so long. "I can't find the crayons," I say. "The last time I saw them, they were on the bar." He immediately enters the second bedroom, rifles through the blankets, and pulls them into view. "The baby and I were playing with them on the bed this morning after you left for work," he replies.

I am flabbergasted. I had been in precisely the right spot, but doubt had thwarted me at the finish line.

But what if we want to *find* something more significant than car keys or bath crayons? What if we wish to find a new job? Or a soulmate? Or a new creative idea? Regardless of what we seek, *finding* always starts the same way.

Send a clear signal of what you want to draw into your life. After that, let the Universe, your Guides, and Trickster take over. Your job is to completely let go of the anxiety around *looking*, as well as attachment to outcome (i.e., overly stringent criteria about *what, when,* and *how* it shows up), and let your energy lead the way.

Like co-creation, *finding* requires alignment. We can't successfully *find* if we're sending mixed signals to the Universe. And *finding* follows all the other rules laid out in Chapter 2—no cop-outs! But *finding* also requires more trust on our part. We're more likely to follow intuitive hits on where to go, who to talk to, or what leads to investigate if we trust the process.

If you are looking for ways to jump-start your Spiritual Path work, you can start *finding* in a library, as I did, or on a walk outside. Even finding while shopping can lead you to an object that opens a door where you thought there was only a wall.

The more we connect with what our heart, soul, and spirit really want, the more often remarkable *finds* turn up in our lives. If we can let go of what we think we want and trust the Universe, our Guides, and our soul to bring us towards what we *really* want, imagine what we might *find*.

Exercise:

Practice Finding. Don't get discouraged if you fail! I cannot emphasize this enough. Consider this a skill you are developing—like shooting a basketball through a hoop. I am terrible at that. I'll never be LeBron James, but I bet if

I practiced, I would get better. Even with lots of practice, I still won't make a basket every time I launch a ball. It's the same with finding.

However, no matter how many times we fail at finding, the silver lining is that this exercise trains us to be more energetically attuned, increasing our ability to receive guidance.

- *Practice Finding at Home*
  - o *Pick something you wish to find, such as a book or keys, and ask for help in finding it from your Guides (and/or Trickster, as your comfort level allows).*
  - o *Reduce your visual receptivity in whatever way you feel safe; closing your eyes halfway or wearing dark sunglasses indoors. Ensure you can see well enough to avoid tripping over things.*
  - o *Shift your attention to your legs and feet and allow them to walk you wherever they want to go.*
  - o *When they stop, see if you feel the urge to pick anything up, turn anything over.*
  - o *If not, notice where your eyes fall.*
  - o *When you get stuck & discouraged (and believe me, unless you really are the LeBron James of finding, you will), distract yourself by doing something unrelated and monotonous that still requires movement (I usually pick the laundry or dishes). Then, while doing the task, see if you feel the thread of finding pick back up.*
  - o *If ideas of potential locations for the object keep occurring to your conscious mind, I find it best to check those and eliminate them first.*
- *Finding in a Library or Bookstore*
  - o *Finding in a library or bookstore can be a great way to open your Path in new directions. Use the same steps as above, but at the library or bookstore.*

- *Finding on a walk*
  - o *Using similar steps to the previous exercises, turn down your visual receptivity (safely!) and allow your feet to walk you where they want to go.*
  - o *Pay special attention at intersections to which direction you feel guided to turn (or not turn)*
  - o *As the directional energy in your legs lessens, turn back up your visual receptivity and notice where you are. Does anything catch your eye?*
  - o *If you work in an urban area, finding on a walk can be a great way to find a new lunch spot!*
- *Finding while Shopping (Shopping can be a* very *satisfying way to practice Finding)*
  - o *Set an intention of what you want to find (for example, a new kitchen table that costs no more than $x)—then allow your energy to lead the way.*
  - o *Do you feel drawn to visit a particular store? To scroll through the options on a specific site? Sometimes just driving around, letting your energy guide you, can lead you to the right retailer.*
  - o *Or maybe you feel drawn to tell your friendship group you're looking for a new table, and someone happens to be getting rid of one.*
- *Finding Someone in a Place*
  - o *The next time you have to meet someone in a public place, try finding them the same way you find an object.*
  - o *Note: Pick a low-stakes scenario, especially the first few times you try it. Avoid using finding in a state of panic like looking for a temporarily misplaced child, as it's just likely to increase your anxiety (unless you've gotten really good at it). As a counterpoint, though, I can think of at least one example of using finding to locate my oldest daughter in Maggie Daley Park when we lost track of her for fifteen minutes. I was so desperate I couldn't think of anything else—it was easier to turn everything off and let my energy take over. Moments after I asked for help, my eyes fell on her just as she exited a slide one hundred feet away.*

18

LOVE YOUS IN DISGUISE

Finding and Healing Soul Wounds

Way back at the turn of the millennium, as I first descended from the spiritual bliss of Initiation phase, a flash of inspiration helped me navigate conflict with my loved ones more effectively. I realized that all the times my parents nagged me about things—wearing a hat when it's cold outside, doing well in school, the importance of being financially stable—their hearts were really telling me, "*I love you.*" These *love yous* came dressed up in many forms, at times completely unrecognizable. So I started calling them "love yous in disguise."[47]

---

[47] Incidentally, when I met the man who was to become my husband, we realized that "love yous in disguise" have a counterpart. When we are acting out in jealousy, or being sulky and withdrawn, or hurt by something the other has said, what our hearts are really saying is "*Love me.*" Love mes can wear particularly scary disguises and are often even harder to see than love yous in disguise. We saw both love yous and love mes as imaginary creatures, donning costumes out of fear. Both creatures turned out to be very helpful in navigating conflict because they reminded us to recognize the love or need for love *first*, and then back out and address the surface issue.

When the Universe pokes at a particularly pervasive soul wound of mine, I find it reassuring to remind myself that these are really love yous from the Universe, wearing uncomfortably scary disguises. We develop soul wounds through our interaction with other people, the world around us, and even our interaction with ourselves. We can sustain soul wounds for years, maybe even lifetimes, without realizing it. It hurts when they're touched, but the Universe taps on them to help us find them and, ultimately, heal them.

X-Ray Vision

Finding our Soul wounds is often a matter of *allowing* ourselves to see them. Whenever we have an outsized emotional reaction to something, it's a clue; an iceberg might be hiding underneath. Once we see a soul wound, we recognize its impact everywhere in our lives. We're baffled how we missed it before.

In the fall of 2014, I went for a life-between-lives regression. In such a session, the therapist directs our consciousness to the place we go *in between* lifetimes. Before approaching the between-lives state, though, she regressed me to my time in the womb and asked me to describe how I felt.

Much to my shock, I erupted in sobs. "I just feel so unwanted," I huffled, when I finally managed to form a few words. The session moved on, but the incident disturbed me, and I brought it up afterward with my then-husband.

"Are you going to talk to your mom about it?" he asked.

I hesitated. As a mother myself, I had suffered from episodes of fear and anxiety during my pregnancy. I had a very loving relationship with my mom; I would hate for her to feel bad over a fleeting instance of regret that my fetal-self had picked up on. Deciding no good could come from discussing it with her, I dismissed the event from my mind.

Six months later, as I walked my daughter's stroller through a small woodsy area, I had a revelation. Working with Trickster had taught me that Soulwork is often hiding in plain sight. Regardless of what my *mom* had been dealing with, my feeling "unwanted" was a valid emotion, and I shouldn't ignore it. That moment in the regression session had been weighty enough for rivers of tears to flow. I needed to explore what that meant *for me*.

Once I opened that door, pieces from other regression sessions began to align with my current existence, and a minor earthquake struck my heart. Feeling "unwanted" had nothing to do with my mom. I had come *into* life with those feelings. In the womb, I *already had them*.

I had hidden this wound from myself, but now I could clearly see its impact splattered across my life. At work, it manifested in an intense dislike of being left out of things: projects, meetings, conversations among friends. I tried not to let those feelings show, of course, but I *felt* them. Sometimes my emotional reaction was strong enough to cause me to act suprisingly standoffish, driving people away rather than bringing them closer. I never understood my behavior at the time. I would think to myself, *Why did I do that?*

Now I knew.

My occasional flirtations with male coworkers made more sense now, too, despite thinking of myself as happily married. I never *thought* of it as flirting, of course; I saw it as "just being friendly." Recognizing my soul wound helped me view this behavior through a different lens. Even before marriage, I had created romantic relationships that revolved around the expression of desire or "wanting." Although I seemed to be functioning just fine on the surface, I could now see all the ways this wound was making a mess of my life.

The most intriguing insight was yet to come, though. I had been reading a book about life-between-life sessions (which had inspired me to go for my own). In one of them, the process of "soul birth" is described as tiny particles of energy emitting from a bright, energetic source. In the middle of a restless night several months later, I dreamt of that glowing cradle of power and felt myself splitting off from it: a miniature golden orb, launching into the darkness.

I woke myself with the wetness of tears. Not happy tears like we sometimes experience at weddings or with childbirth; this was gut-wrenching anguish.

I sat up in bed, confused. *What the heck is wrong with me?* I wondered. *Why am I crying about this? There's nothing sad or disturbing about imagining tiny sparks of energy being born into souls.*

And then a tiny voice whispered like a soft whirlwind out of the abyss. *"Why didn't God want me?"*

Wait. *What?*

A series of emotions rushed forth on the heels of that quiet question that I would translate as: *Why did he kick me out? Why did he send me to Earth? Why didn't God want me to be part of his energy anymore?*

I'll probably never know if it was a 3 a.m. delusion or truth from the very core of my being, but for the first time, it occurred to me that I might have been carrying this "unwanted" wound for longer than my last past life or two. What if I'd been holding onto it since the *birth of my soul*?

Regardless of the wound's genesis, what a remarkable gift to have *seen* it and finally have the opportunity to heal it. I could feel Trickster's revelatory hand at work: the magician, pulling back the curtain. If I hadn't been studying Trickster and starting to recognize the signs of hiding something from myself, it would never have occurred to me that there was anything to see here at all.

But now that I had seen the damage, I had no idea how to *fix* it. A wound based on feeling unwanted seemed to direct me back to how *others* felt about me—something I might influence but couldn't really control. With my years of experience navigating Soulwork, I knew immediately that seeking out ways to feel wanted wouldn't help me heal. That was the subconscious strategy I had been employing for years. It had only brought me unhappiness and disruption. But if generating a feeling of being wanted wasn't the cure for feeling *unwanted*, what was?

To take a crack at the problem, I tried paying attention to all the times the wound flared up. I learned this skill working through past Soulwork and figured it would offer valuable data. "Luckily," I had lots of opportunities for observation. I remember one occasion where I ended a project status meeting and noticed some team members hanging around. "You guys don't have to stay here," I said. "You're free to leave."

One of them laughed lightheartedly and said, "Actually, we have a meeting in this room now, so *you're* the one who has to leave."

It had been said without malice, yet I felt a familiar twinge in my heart: the whimpering of my unwanted wound. Surprisingly, even such a small thing as that could wake it. Although I hadn't yet *healed* the wound, awareness of it allowed me to consciously *choose* how to respond. Where previously I might have silently sulked or glared and stalked off, instead I could laugh off my coworker's comment while internally acknowledging a chord had been struck.

Even if we can't instantly heal our wounds, increasing our awareness of them allows us to act more mindfully when they become inflamed. Being present with our emotional reactions won't prevent us from having them, but can help us minimize their potential for destruction in our external lives.

I stayed with perception for almost a year, actively watching for healing techniques but not really finding anything. On the upside, choosing how to respond when my injury enflamed enabled me to make positive changes in my life and relationships. And the more I acknowledged and honored my internal pain, the less intense the reactions were when it surfaced. What would once have caused a five-alarm emotional fire now resulted in more of a disappointed shrug.

My first lead on healing arrived with the first Sonia Choquette *Teacher Training* workshop I attended in person. In one of our sessions, Sonia talked about finding a soul wound while walking the Camino de Santiago de Compostela. Instead of judging and shunning that part of herself, she embraced it, telling her wound, "When I dance, I dance for you."

Inspiration struck. While I had been compassionate with myself about my wound, I hadn't really been *embracing* it. I pivoted from a place of tolerance to one of love. I, too, dedicated dances to my wounded self. I celebrated the moments when my wound surfaced, and I consciously chose not to nurse it with the junk food of instant gratification. *It doesn't matter if I'm not wanted in a particular place, or time, or situation, or by a particular person,* I told myself, *I'm happy to be me and proud of how I've grown.*

And I meant it.

That process helped me heal my "unwanted" wound to the point where it didn't even flutter when my then-husband left me for another woman. Yet, I developed some additional healing techniques in recovering from my divorce that I wish I had had before.

Hearts in a Sling

We tend to treat our emotional wounds as if healing will happen naturally, in the background, over time. But my "unwanted" soul wound suggests otherwise. I might have been carrying it for decades, and still, its influence seeped into every corner of my life. Even when we *do* approach our emotional wounds, there's often a focus on who or what *caused* the damage. But this is like focusing our attention on the stairs after we've tumbled down them. Understanding why we fell can help us avoid additional harm. But that knowledge does nothing to heal the bumps, bruises, and breaks obtained in the incident. Beyond our first few minutes in the emergency room, we want the doctor to focus on our injuries, not the cause. The *last* thing we want to hear as we're writhing in pain is, "About those stairs...."

What if it's the same for emotional wounds? For some physical wounds, like animal bites or burns, understanding the cause does help determine the treatment. Still, I suspect we overemphasize the importance of external causes when addressing internal injuries. Accusing my mother of "not wanting" me while I was in the womb would have *impeded* the healing of my "unwanted" wound and may have caused her unnecessary guilt and grief. If focusing on external causes is helping you, keep doing that. Just don't ignore any actual *healing* your heart requires.

But how, then, do we *heal* an emotional wound?

In keeping with our comparison thus far, what if we treated our emotional wounds more like physical wounds? How do we heal a physical wound?

With bodily injury, we're often instructed to be cautious when *using* the affected part of our anatomy. Certain activities may be off-limits, and certain movements might cause us pain. Depending on how severe the wound is, the healing process could take weeks, months, maybe more.

When we feel discomfort, we tend to want to escape it. More often than not, we reach for numbness. But numbness alone doesn't *heal* anything. We might take enough painkillers to allow us to keep walking on our broken leg, for example, but we're likely to hinder rather than help its healing. We might even make the break worse. Numbness is billed as the *absence* of sensation, but it's still a type of experience and not necessarily a pleasant one.

In preparation for giving birth, I learned quite a bit about pain. Typically, bodily pain tells us that something is *wrong*, but with childbirth, the pain is a side effect of our body opening and making space to deliver a new being into the world. The pain doesn't signal a problem; it's part of the process. Perhaps it is the same with rebirthing ourselves.

Regardless of why our hearts are hurting, we may be more sensitive when engaging in activities where we are emotionally invested, whether romantic, familial, or work-related. We need to give our hearts a rest and lots of compassion when recovering from emotional trauma.

HEART HEALING MEDICINE

In addition to a time-out, we may need medication or physical therapy to heal damage to our physical body. With our emotional wounds, the twin treatments are *Comfort* and *Joy*.

In one of Sonia's teacher-training sessions, she taught us how to actively bring joy into our lives. We sat in small groups based on her instruction and took turns calling out activities that lightened our hearts: *Sledding! Dancing! Pillow Fights!*

One year later, going through my divorce, I recognized that there were times when I couldn't get to Joy. The climb felt too steep, my despair too deep.

Enter Comfort.

Remembering the Joy exercise inspired me to ask myself what brought me comfort. If I couldn't get to joy, maybe self-comfort was a more achievable goal. Turning to a blank page in my healing journal, I started a list: *a mug of hot tea in the morning, fluffy socks, a heated shower or relaxing bath, snuggling up in blankets with a good book, a warm hug from my daughters, coloring an intricate sketch with glittery gel pens.* I listed comfort foods, soothing music, as well as friends and family I could count on to bring me solace when at my lowest points.

I recognized that Comfort could be a doorway to Joy. A heart full of Joy is potent healing medicine, but we need to be in an emotional state where we can actually *feel* it: sometimes, that requires Comfort first.

Exercise: *Divide a piece of paper down the middle to create two columns. On one side, list the things that bring you comfort—things that might make sadness, anxiety, or fear more tolerable, for example. On the other side, list things that bring you joy—activities, shows, music, etc.—that make you laugh-out-loud happy and generate a feeling of lightness in your being. It's okay to list big things, like a vacation, but try to also list small things—like a cup of your favorite coffee or taking a quick walk—that are easy to fit in your life in those moments of immediate need.*

Now, put your finger on each item on the Comfort list and actively think about doing it or enjoying it (whatever it is). Notice how this makes you feel inside. Next, do the same with the items on the Joy side.

These are your personal tools. Remember to actively use them whenever you need comfort and/or joy in your life. Try to incorporate at least one small comfort or joy item from your list into your daily routine. Even if you're prevented from doing these activities at present, remember that it brings you some comfort and joy just to think *about them and plan for a time when you can* do *them.*

AN OUNCE OF PREVENTION

We also need to take better care of our hearts in general. If you first thought of cardiovascular disease when you read that, it proves my point. We give almost no time or care to our emotional well-being unless something is drastically wrong. Even when we *do* attend to our emotions, we direct our efforts towards "managing" them like they're children. Our rational mind is, of course, the parent. Yet our emotional being is more core to who we are than our rational selves—we had emotions far earlier than we could reason. So when we attack our emotions, we're attacking the purest version of ourselves that we have.

In January of 2020, I met a guy who seemed kind of perfect for me. He was smart, funny, kind, easy to talk to, and there appeared to be great chemistry between us. Still healing from my divorce, my heart warned me not to get involved. But I did anyway. We briefly explored a friends-with-benefits type of relationship, but his interest blew hot and cold, and I couldn't comfortably navigate the emotional uncertainty. Unsure of how to handle the situation, I pulled us back to friendship, telling myself that was a safer place to be.

Except my heart didn't really want to be friends with this guy; she wished for something more. Thus followed nearly a year of my attempting to openly and honestly be friends while secretly hoping he would develop romantic feelings for me and desire a closer connection. When that didn't happen, I got crushed over and over again.

It's okay, I told myself. *I just need to stop* having *these feelings—then we can* really *be* just *friends.* So I went to war with my own emotions.

Meanwhile, I sought guidance from my Guides on finding *real* love again. They kept directing me back to *self-love, self-love, self-love.* I was annoyed with this advice. I already devoted time to meditating, playing, making time for what I enjoy, practicing self-compassion, and pampering myself. Wasn't I *already doing* self-love?

At some point during all the teeth-gnashing over Mr. January, though, I realized that it was *not* self-loving of me to stay in a one-sided connection. Instead of attacking my feelings, I needed to allow them to be what they were. My actions were setting my heart up for perpetual pain. To truly practice self-love, I had to stop doing that. So I stepped back from the friendship, allowing it to naturally dissipate.

A few months after this revelation, in December of 2020, I met someone who seemed even better for me.

We met several times and talked for hours on the phone. Mr. December's ideas pushed me to examine areas of my life and pieces of myself that I had let stagnate. And through our discussions, my world expanded. Mr. December periodically recorded his thoughts and feelings in an online blog that revealed his heart—raw and beautiful. *I have to stop reading this blog,* I told myself, *or I am going to fall in love with this guy...and that would be a disaster at this early stage.* So I stopped.

When he visited, he would fix little things that weren't working quite right, just by nature, without my even asking. It was adorable. *Ugh,* I thought, *too late, I already love him.*

The only problem? He was in love with someone else.

And when she came back to him (who wouldn't?), he broke things off with me. He seemed to genuinely want to stay friends, though, and I was so tempted to say yes.

Except I knew better by now.

And after twenty-five years of doing this work, I knew this was an opportunity for me to demonstrate to the Universe that I had learned my lesson.

Love Yous in disguise.

So, this time I said no.

It hurt so much more than I expected. I had lost not only the physical connection of the relationship, but all those great discussions as well. In the beginning, I assuaged myself that if I still wanted to be friends with him in six months, and I could do so without expecting anything more, I could reach out. Eventually, I had to release that idea, though. I clutched it like a lifeline, preventing me from fully releasing him.

Still, this go-around, I could apply lessons from prior experience. I knew the pain *would* get better. And now, I had an arsenal of tools and techniques to ease my suffering.

I'm getting pretty good at handling heartbreak, I reflected.

Which made me less afraid of it.

Instead of my heart wanting to shut down, she felt comfortable staying open because she could finally trust that I would take better care of her. Through the pain, I gained clarity on how I had also set myself up for injury in *this* situation. While Mr. December made himself readily available for conversation or meetings when I reached out, I almost always initiated contact. A week would go by without even a hello. *Guys who are genuinely interested will* want *to connect*, I reminded myself. I ignored those warning signs, though, and dove headfirst into heartache.

There were aspects of his behavior, too, that I suspected were *not* a good fit for me. I couldn't understand how my rational mind knew this, yet I still hung on emotionally. Instead of attacking my emotions this time, though, I accepted and tried to understand them. I used an exercise taught by Sonia Choquette, *my head says/my heart says/my soul says/my spirit says,* to help myself dig deeper into this discrepancy.

When I asked myself, "Why am I still hanging on to this?" my head said, "Because we had good discussions. I enjoyed the physical connection tremendously. He was funny and fun, and we seemed to be interested in a lot of the same subjects."

My heart said, "I can't imagine finding anyone better than this."

My soul said, "I'm afraid I'll ultimately have to choose between being alone or settling for someone really interested and attracted to me when I don't feel the same about them."

But the real breakthrough came from my spirit.

My spirit said, "You know the Universe can send you a phenomenal match, right? Haven't you seen the Universe deliver exactly what you want time and time again in your life? You've done your work and continue to do it. So why don't you think you deserve that?"

At which point I realized—I *do* deserve it. I have done and continue to do my Soulwork. I know how the Universe operates. If what I wish for isn't showing up, it's because *I'm* not aligned: something within *me* is sending mixed signals to the Universe.

Which brought the question back to me: "*Why am I saying no to love?*"

It's a funny thing, writing about my own Soulwork. Sometimes clarity blooms in the spaces between the writing process. I didn't understand the source of my misalignment in the previous iteration of this manuscript. Now I do.

Subconsciously, I had been thinking of a new romantic relationship a bit like a reward. Having gone through all this deep healing and growth, secretly, I expected the Universe to *reward* me with the "right" person. (Presumably, with whom I could ride off into the sunset, right?) But a relationship is about *two* people, with all their history and potential, coming together. A relationship isn't a prize; it's a growth opportunity.

Well-functioning relationships tend to have two modes; stasis and growth. Stasis isn't inherently unhealthy, and many happy, healthy relationships operate in a comfortable cadence for years. But if we intend to avoid repeating an old pattern, we have to *grow into* a new one. I've spent two hard years working through the demanding and relentless Soulwork surrounding my divorce. (Not to mention all the Soulwork of being *in* my marriage.) My heart is exhausted.

Even though I am sometimes lonely for romantic companionship, part of my heart is telling me *I don't want to be vulnerable. I don't want to trust or let anyone in right now. I just want to* feel safe and at peace *for a while.* Yet, to be *in* the kind of relationship I wanted, my only choice was more growth. Hence, misalignment. My mind, body, and part of my heart want one thing, but the rest of my heart wants another.

In some ways, I was secretly hoping the "right" person could convince the reluctant part of my heart to get on board. But that just risks more co-dependency (Rule#5—the Universe doesn't support cop-outs—remember?). The only person who can make my heart *truly* feel safe and cared for is *me.*

When we stop fighting our hearts and start caring for them instead, our deepest healing can begin.

Exercise: *Think of any areas of your life that currently cause you pain. (If you can't think of anything current, lucky you! It's okay to use an example from the past just to try out the exercise).*

- *Write down any repeated behaviors you engaged in that created or exacerbated that pain.*
   o *For example, repeatedly trying to please a demanding boss, approval-seeking behavior toward an emotionally unavailable loved one (parent, sibling, spouse, child, etc.)*
- *Imagine if you could just* stop *doing that same behavior. (I don't mean stop going to work or stop talking to your mom, here.) Instead, just let go of the specific behavior or expectation that brings pain.*
- *If you still feel emotionally attached to a specific outcome, try using Sonia's head says/heart says exercise to reveal what might be hiding underneath the painful behavior.*

19

ADVENTURES IN FAILURE

The Often Bumpy Road of Bringing Our Gifts into the World

I am not famous. I have not written any best-selling books or made millions of dollars helping thousands of people. How can I possibly give advice on bringing our gifts into the world successfully? I can't. So this chapter doesn't tackle triumph; its focus is failure. If that seems like a Trickster sleight of hand, it is. Congratulations on spotting it! You're learning how to recognize Trickster energy at work. Just because it's a shift in perspective, though, doesn't mean there aren't valuable lessons to learn about the rewarding process of bringing our gifts into the world here, too.

As children in school, we are most often taught about the accomplishments of those who have come before us. When we learn about and engage with failure, it's almost always cast in a negative light. Of course, we study successful people *because* they have changed our world somehow—that's what brought them renown. Pythagoras gave the world his illustrious theorem; Thomas Edison gave us the incandescent lightbulb.

Even when we finally graduate from school and make our own way in the world, what we see most often on the news and in the media—at least through a positive lens—is other people's success.

Sure, some highly talented, lucky people catch a break with their earliest endeavors. For most of us, though, even the most prominent among us, lifetime achievement is built on a backbone of experimentation and failure. We do a tremendous service to the children growing into future leaders to teach them more about that. Besides, one of the most significant advantages of anonymity is the opportunity to fail in the dark. I'm sure we can all think of individuals who found early success but had their mistakes forever after play out in a public forum.

Only in a college philosophy class—not a math class—did I learn that Pythagoras also had a lesser-known "crystal sphere" theory. He speculated that our solar system's planets were attached to concentric crystal orbs. Periodically, these would clink together, explaining the "beautiful music" he sometimes heard. Living with pleasant ambient music only you can hear is an enviable experience, but we have now sent enough probes into space to know that Pythagoras's crystal sphere idea is just plain wrong. Yet, we can still appreciate the magnificence of $a^2 + b^2 = c^2$.

And it was only in watching the HBO documentary *The Inventor,* itself a cautionary tale, that I learned how many times Edison failed to produce the incandescent light bulb before eventually succeeding.

The average novel or screenplay might go through ten to twenty drafts before seeing sunlight, *if it ever does.* With this book, each chapter went through several drafts, chapters have been rearranged into completely different parts of the book, and the whole book has gone through multiple revisions.

My Guides were laying out these markers of others' failures as stepping stones. When I was writing a blog no one was reading, or sinking hours of time, energy, and love into a book that might suffer a quiet and unremarkable death, I could remember that so many others have been down this road. The act of creation isn't just about success; it's about failure, too.

It returns me to the T-shirt I spotted while coming home with take-out: *Doubt kills more dreams than failure ever could.* At the root of that doubt is *fear—fear* of failure kills our creative spirit as much as, or more than, actual failure. Maybe we're afraid of failure because we're incubated in the stories of others' successes. When failure makes news, it's colossal, only adding to our anxiety.

THANK YOU, NEXT

Google's first definition of failure is simply "lack of success." It's nearly identical to the first definitions listed by dictionary.com and the Cambridge Dictionary and the second for Merriam-Webster.

In Alberto Villoldo's book *The Four Insights,* he shares a Zen story about the highs and lows experienced by a farming family. Every time they encounter a perceived adverse event, their neighbors would say something like, "What rotten luck!" and the farmer would respond, "Good luck, bad luck—who knows." When that seemingly undesirable event results in a perceived positive outcome, the neighbors would exclaim, "What great luck!" but the farmer would only respond, "Good luck, bad luck—who knows." The wheel of fortune continues to turn, and the story's message is clear: with each perceived negative and positive event in our lives, we can't really know where it will lead.[48]

Yes, failure can come with massive damage: public humiliation, significant loss of funds, career setbacks, and even legal troubles. But even mammoth mistakes can lay the groundwork for eventual accomplishment. In the mid-eighties, Steve Jobs was fired from Apple only to return a decade later and lead the company to become one of the world's most

---

[48] Villoldo, 173-4

recognized and idolized brands. One of Bill Gates's early companies failed. Walt Disney's early cartoon characters, including Mickey Mouse, were rebuffed by studios. And J. K. Rowling's popular work *Harry Potter and the Sorcerer's Stone* was rejected several times before finally being accepted by a publisher.

In December of 2019, *Harvard Business Review* podcast *The Tipping Point between Failure and Success* featured research on failure from Associate Professor Dashun Wang at Kellogg School of Management. His work followed the careers of postgraduates who had or hadn't won research grants early on. The researchers had embarked on their study expecting those early awards to act as a catalyst for an increasingly widening career gap between the initial winners and their losing peers.

What they found in the process, though, was something quite surprising. Although many grant winners *did* end up with fruitful careers, some students who had *failed* to win a grant also became high achievers. In some cases, the early losers were more productive and their work more influential than those who had beat them out initially.

The research of Wang and his associates showed that if a graduate student failed early on but continued to try, learning and tweaking as they went, they usually found success. Even more importantly, if the time between successive attempts reduced with each effort, the student eventually emerged victorious.

So, when is failure absolute, and when is it just a step away from triumph? Regardless of how the outside world treats our contributions, the answer to that question ultimately comes from us. In other words, failure is only "lack of success" when *we* allow it to be. If we allow an unsuccessful experiment to keep us down, we won't ever succeed.

Don't Just Talk a Bad Game, Play One

But perhaps you already know all this. The value of failure is discussed more frequently these days, and we've all come across at least one anecdote of how an early disappointment led to ultimate attainment. I've heard the term "fail fast" bandied about at work; maybe you have too. Perhaps, then, the challenge is—do we embody it? One of the most impactful lessons I've learned on my own Spiritual Path is about the vast gap between understanding and execution. It's one thing to understand something, more challenging to put it into practice.

"In a choice between winning and losing, we choose winning every time," Wang says.

We talk about failure, but how often do we risk it? And not just in a family board game or a friendly ping-pong match where losing is safe and, at least occasionally, expected. How often do we risk failure in something we *really* care about? We don't have to paint a canvas and stick it on our front lawn; risking loss can be something as simple as initiating a difficult conversation with someone we love. Or giving honest feedback to a friend versus hiding behind a "little white lie." Or confronting a coworker or boss if they're out of line instead of keeping our mouths shut. Or being more open about who we are (if we're concealing ourselves for social or professional ease).

If that seems too intense, we don't have to start there. (Although, pay attention to your emotional responses to those ideas. I am.)

To become more acclimated to failure, perhaps one of the best things we can do for ourselves is to regularly seek out other people's failures. Remember the study of the Duncker candle insight task from Chapter 4? The group who watched blooper reels succeeded at a rate of 58%, surpassing all others by a wide margin. So, watch blooper reels. Stream *Nailed It* on Netflix and witness amateur bakers attempt and fail to bake incredible creations in a whimsically humorous setting. Find interviews where now-famous people talk about their fumbles on the path to success. Listen to songs that you *don't* like by artists that you *do* like to remind yourself that not *everything* they create is a hit.

Surround yourself with failure, and your own will be less scary.

Don't Start at the Finish Line

With some notable exceptions (building construction comes to mind), we're surrounded by *finished* projects.

Seek out examples of popular and profitable work in early prototypes and in an unfinished state to liberate yourself from seeing your own efforts only through the lens of the "final draft."

Don't (Only) Look Up

I mentioned this at the beginning of this chapter, but it bears repeating with a slightly different spin. Not only are we surrounded by finished work, but we focus on people at the top of their game. When we watch sports, we're seeing athletes at the top of their game. When we read a *New York Times* best-selling novel, we're reading a book by an author at the top of their game. When we go to an art museum, we see artists at the top of their game. When we watch a blockbuster movie, we're seeing actors and directors at the top of their game.

If you're a beginning creator (like me!), immerse yourself in examples of people *not* at the top of their game. YouTube is a gold mine of people just starting out. Watch someone's first fitness video. Read another self-published book (besides this one). Go to an amateur film festival. Cheer in the stands for an intramural sport. We don't start creating at the top of our game, and it may take us a while to get there. Trickster reminds us that we're not trapped in an either-or; either we find epic success or colossal failure. Many exemplary careers are built in the range in between.

And here I feel Trickster poking me in the side, reminding me that we're knee-deep in a chapter about bringing gifts into the world, and we haven't even asked the two most fundamental questions: What is a gift, and what does it mean to bring it into the world?

We may think first of tangible skills, asking ourselves, *"What am I good at?"* Writing? Singing? Programming? Teaching? We might wonder how we can practice and refine these talents and skills to make a living doing them. That's what it means to bring a gift into the world, right?

But what if we don't love to do the things we're good at? Sure, we might enjoy how it feels when someone tells us how good we are, but what if that were to stop? What if, instead, people said we were terrible. Would we still enjoy doing it? Would it still be a "gift"?

What if we crafted a career doing something we love and also happen to be brilliant at—like performing? Does this mean our entire life becomes defined by that solitary talent? When others rise up to replace us, is our life over? What if we simply want to move on and try something new?

We can resolve some of these issues by broadening our idea of what a gift is. Perhaps we have a talent for bringing people together, for example. No, not as a matchmaker, but for gatherings, parties, building a community. Making people feel good or listening without judgment might be our forte. Maybe we're apt at giving straight-up, no-nonsense advice. It might be too much for some, but for others, it might provide the nudge needed to make real, lasting change. We might have a knack for describing complex things in easy-to-understand ways.

A gift is a *positive expression of the soul*. Bringing them into the world, then, is *allowing those gifts to express themselves as part of our daily lives.* In working through our Soulwork, we will discover many gifts. Navigating a challenging Dark Night of the Soul might increase our capacity for compassion. We might, then, bring that compassion into the world to support a child in despair or bridge a stalemate between two opposing parties. We may develop a flair for being our true selves. Witnessing our authenticity might grant others the courage to be more genuine.

We may never move millions of people with an inspired work of genius, but we can celebrate the contributions we bring into the world every day. That is the effortless part of expressing gifts—the part that comes naturally as we navigate our Soulwork. We can focus so intently on a single project we're working on, we overlook all the other ways we touch, inspire, and uplift those around us. Even a single sentence said to the right person at the right moment can have massive impact.

Would you rather have a profoundly positive influence on the lives of twenty people or fifteen minutes of fleeting fame among twenty million? I realize those are not the only two possibilities that exist, but for most of us, the first option is within reasonable reach.

THE GIFT-GIVING TREE

Sometimes the soul moves in a profound and life-changing way that we feel deeply, but we're not sure *how* to manifest. This is when we might have an idea for opening a restaurant because we're called to bring people together around food. This is when we might want to write a book to share our ideas with the world. This is when we might want to start a business to solve a problem we see others struggling with or that we have grappled with ourselves.

These are all gifts, too. We might pour many hours of our heart and soul into these gifts. Bringing them into the world is far more complicated.

I started bringing my spiritual process into the world ten years ago by writing a blog read by almost no one. I twice tried to start businesses that never really got off the ground, and I wrote 70% of a book (not this one), to which the primary response of the friends and family I could cajole into reading it was confusion.

Throughout the book, I've offered many reasons why Trickster acts as a powerful guide on our Spiritual Path, but I find him an especially essential companion in the creative process. Trickster sometimes (often) screws up, but he also brings transformative change to the world. Raven eats his family out of house and home, getting booted from his spirit village. But as a consequence, he brings our world into being. Coyote steals a glowing orb from the Buffalo people and gives us the moon. Anansi breaks the pot containing all the world's wisdom, making it available to everyone. Maui introduces death into the world, but also the fire through which we cook our food; the same fire that anthropologists believe may have catapulted humans to higher levels of consciousness. In the act of creating, some of our ideas, some of our productions, will be shit. But Trickster reminds us that we use that same substance to fertilize new growth. We never know what will change the world.

On the path to bringing our gifts into being, large or small, we will bump into our Soulwork in the form of skills and, sometimes, obstacles. Through it all, it's good to remember that we have *many, many* gifts we bring into the world every day and that the failure of an idea to take hold in the public consciousness does not translate into the failure of an idea for *us*. Guidance—and experience—don't have to be transformative for everyone to be transformative for *us*. Merely in the act of trying, and trying, and *trying*, we become more than what we were before.

I return to the advice Freya whispered in my ear three years ago. It applies for all of us: *just keep going.*

We all have gifts we bring into the world. We start by cultivating and appreciating our simple gifts because, through these, our larger contributions to humanity are revealed. How we choose to express those gifts is a matter for personal exploration.

We've introduced Trickster as guardian of the boundary and the embodiment of duality. When we look at this challenge through the lens of duality, we recognize that both success and failure are really just *change*. If we perceive the change as positive, we tend to view it as a success—"What great luck!" If we perceive the change as unfavorable, we tend to see it as failure. But none of us *really* know where all these successes and failures will lead.

No one really decides what the next frontiers of science, technology, art, or thought will be. Some breakthrough happens—maybe in a garage, maybe in someone's head—and it builds from that small space until it takes over the world. Of course, it doesn't always happen that way. Innovation can come out of traditional institutions, and the world is littered with small-scale broken dreams. Regardless of the source of change, though, no consortium of human affairs gets together across the world (or even within a single community) to decide exactly how to change from year to year. Change is all there is, and somehow, with more or less enthusiasm, we adapt.

This is not to say that animals don't adapt to their environments. They do. However, nowhere in the animal kingdom do we see dramatic change at the scale and pace we find among human beings. Think of how much the human house has evolved in the last thousand years. It's difficult to point to a similar magnitude of innovation in, let's say, the domiciles of squirrels. Not only that, but for humans, the change we must adapt to is often self-created. This brings us to a revelation about the human experience.

Humans, more than any other species, consciously build on what came before.

And all those blocks from the past (both successes and failures) give us *lots* of material to work with. We find freedom in our creative expression by embracing the idea that each contribution we make is neither a fully fleshed-out pyramid nor a pile of sand—it's a block, a building block we use to build together.

Exercises:

- *Make a list of your everyday gifts, the gifts you bring—or could bring—into the world just by being you, just through regular interactions with others, and through your engagement with the world.*
- *Find and engage with a show, a podcast, a piece of written material, or some other medium that exemplifies positive failure (i.e., don't focus on a failure that ruined someone's life; find a failed experiment that ultimately led to success). Journal about your feelings and anything you learned from engaging with this material.*
- *Journal, sketch, or talk out loud to someone else or yourself (perhaps even with your phone recorder on, as that can be helpful) about your own failures and what you've learned from them. If you choose to do this exercise with someone else, set the expectations up front that you're not looking for them to "fix" or "reassure" or provide feedback (maybe they could if you think this would be helpful). You just need someone to listen as you process through previous failures and how they have contributed to the person you are today.*

20

Storytelling

Finding Freedom from Our Own Narrative

We're a month into the COVID-19 shutdown of early 2020 and I'm doing my best to embrace enforced solitude. One of the spiritual development projects I've been working on when my ex has the kids is developing an archetype map of my life using the Carolyn Myss and Pete Occhiogrosso board game *Sacred Contracts: The Journey.* I see this as yet another lens I can use to self-study and approach the project with a sense of curiosity about what I might learn.

The "game" comes with a deck of seventy-four archetype cards and a board modeled on the astrological wheel chart: a big circle divided into twelve sections, called houses, each represented by a zodiac sign. In *Sacred Contracts: The Journey,* players select an archetype card to represent each astrological house, which translates to an area of our lives: self, communication, relationships, life purpose, and so on.

One of the cards that turned up surprised me: the Storyteller. My former husband could spin a bedtime yarn that held our two girls enthralled or in stitches. On the occasions I couldn't avoid a turn, I would ramble and fumble over characters, events, and plot. I could never quite knit the pieces together in a compelling way. Despite all my enthusiasm for Trickster, the consummate storyteller, I am woefully inadequate at this skill. But, I believe the card came up for me, not to emphasize the yarns we spin for others but to call attention to the tales we tell ourselves.

In walking the Spiritual Path, surrounded by a sea of meaning, it's easy to be seduced by the story: the larger narrative of life, the Universe, and everything, yes, but also our own personal story. I'm both attracted to and repelled by the "story" of my divorce, for example.

There are so many ways to infuse that event with meaning. Maybe it's me growing past my unwanted wound, maybe it's karma for my affair, maybe I needed more space to grow, but of course, that makes it all about me.

Maybe he was resistant to growth. Maybe he was running away from happiness. Maybe he was running *toward* happiness. Maybe he needed to break out of the marriage for his own growth.

Maybe all of these stories are true.

Maybe none of them are.

When disturbing events shift the center of gravity in our lives, toppling the perceived reality we've painstakingly erected, of course, we want to understand, "Why?" How can we make sure this *never* happens again if we're unclear why it happened in the first place?

When we're healing, we find comfort in meaning, and while we do, the stories that help us heal can be the oxygen that keeps us breathing. There's no shame in leaning into that and letting it surround us like a warm blanket of loving care.

The trick is to know when to let those stories go.

One of my favorite Huston Smith quotes sums this up perfectly: "If we ask ourselves whether there is anything wrong with toys, our answer must be: On the contrary, the thought of children without them is sad. Even sadder, however, is the prospect of adults who fail to develop interests more significant than dolls and trains."[49]

Stories are a bit like crutches. When we break a leg, we may need them to walk, but part of healing is recognizing when it's time to put them away and stand on our own. This is not to say we need to have *no* story. But, if part of our Soulwork is to examine where we are bound, we need to be willing to look at *all* the ways we are bound. We fall for a Trickster trap if we allow ourselves to be bound by our own story.

Trickster provides an excellent model for the duality of storytelling. When we surrender to the mood of a movie or the magic of a good book, it can transport us, teach us, and, in some cases, change the way we look at the world forever. At the same time, we need to be able to cultivate enough distance to recognize that, in the end, it's just a story.

When a master storyteller catches us in their web, it can unearth deep parts of our souls, effecting powerful transformation. Stories can teach us how to navigate challenging life situations. But stories can be more than just comforting—they can be dangerous, too. The conspiracy theories used to justify violence are stories just as much as the silver screen movies that captivate us.

To become tied to a particular narrative about the world makes us ideological. And the more ideological we become, the less data-driven, the more we try to make data fit our story (or ignore it entirely) rather than revising our story to acknowledge the data. If we're too attached to our tale, we risk becoming so lost in a narrative that we no longer feel responsible for our own choices.

---

[49] Huston Smith, *The World's Religions* (San Francisco: Harper Collins, 1991), 17

One quick and easy way to tell if we've handed over control of our choices to a story is to notice anytime we rationalize an action or decision based on an *external* factor. "I do this because he/she/they/the world, etc."

For example, I stay in a job I hate because:

- My family needs me to.
- There isn't a better one out there for me (i.e., the world won't hand me a better job).
- Society expects me to be the breadwinner of the family.

Versus, I stay in a job I hate because:

- I'm worried it's selfish to challenge the current family dynamic to meet my own happiness and fulfillment needs.
- I'm afraid I *won't* find a better job.
- I'm afraid of what others will think of me if I don't have a job or have a significantly less lucrative or high-profile job than my partner.

In the first list of reasons, we project ownership of our choices, and ultimately our lives, onto someone or something else, perhaps because that makes it a little easier for us to avoid taking uncomfortable action. In the second list, we've taken ownership of the insecurities, worries, and fears that drive the decisions we make. And, although we may still make those same selections, at least *we're* clear about why we did so and about what fears and insecurities our choices feed within us.

Fortunately, stories have a mental and emotional hold on us, not a physical one. We can liberate ourselves from our stories without dismantling our life.

When we release our stories, we accept that life isn't always a neatly defined narrative. This lesson arrived for me with the birth of my second child. I've always found it a fun coincidence that my birthday is December 10th at 7:15 in the morning, while my younger sister's birthday is April 10th at 7:15 at night. I used to joke that this is why we're different as night and day.

My own oldest child was born on April 9th, so I was delighted to discover that the due date for my youngest would be December 9th. The exact opposite configuration of my sister and myself. But December 9th came and went with no baby. Somewhat disappointed, I consoled myself in bed that night with the idea that my youngest might be born on my birthday. It would be fun to share a birthday with my youngest child. But December 10th came and went with no baby.

The morning of the 11th dawned with nary a labor pain to speak of, and I started to wonder if this baby would *ever* come out. Then I remembered that it was 2014, and she might be born on the 13th. *12/13/14,* I thought, *What a cool birthday to have.* It would be the last opportunity of the century for a birthday like that.

But my daughter had other plans. She was born at 5:37 a.m. on the morning of the 12th. It was her very first statement to me, *"You will not write my story, mom. I will. And it doesn't have to fit any fanciful pre-conceived notions, either."*

In *Trickster Makes This World*, Lewis Hyde notes that even the most nourishing food becomes scraps we scrape into the garbage (or waste we flush down the toilet). Thus, reminding us that even the most nourishing, precious elements in our lives eventually offer us an exercise in letting go, an opportunity for release.

At times, our stories provide the scaffolding on which we build our future, and we can embrace our story while it serves us well. But if we don't let it go when it's time, we may find ourselves serving our story instead—breathing life into it, feeding it, propping it up. In doing so, we risk losing ourselves.

Even if this happens, though, we need not fear, for Trickster will surely offer a hand to pull the rug from underneath us. And when we finally find our feet again, we'll realize that the Path again beckons, and our Guides stand at the ready for us to journey once more.

THE WOMAN WITH
NO STORY

(a story inspired by the Paiute tale, *Coyote-Giving*[50])

One afternoon
while Coyote was trying to sleep
he heard a loud wailing.

He put his hands over his ears and tried to ignore it,
but it only got louder.

He considered the problem.
He could give up his sleeping spot,
but he was reluctant to do this.

So,
annoyed,
he followed the sound to a woman crying.

She was bawling and moaning and generally feeling sorry for herself.

"Look here,"
he said,
"What's all this ruckus when a body is trying to take an afternoon nap?"

[50] Richard Erdoes and Alfonso Ortiz, *American Indian Trickster Tales* (New York: Penguin Books, 1998), 32

"I do not have a story."
She sniffled, looking up at him through puffy eyes.
"Everyone has a story. Why don't I have a story?"

Coyote sighed.
"If I *give* you a story, will you stop this incessant noise and *go away?*"

Swollen eyes filled with hope,
she nodded.

So, Coyote gave her a story
and she went away.

She followed the story
with delight and wonder.
On its path, she discovered many things about the Universe
and herself.

But one day, as she was following the story along,
she found something on her path she did not expect.

Coyote.

He seemed as surprised to see her as she was to see him,
and as they explained how they both came to arrive at the same point at just that time,
Coyote realized that instead of giving her a *new* story
He had given her
his story.

But a story given belongs as much to its new
owner as it does to the original,
and by now
their paths were so tangled up together they
could never be separate again.

Coyote grumbled half-heartedly,
"Now I will never be free of you, infernal woman."
But she only smiled serenely.

She told him of all the amazing things she had learned on her journey,
the boundaries she had crossed,
the incredible things she had found,
the truths that had been revealed to her,
the weighty sadness she had released.

She promised not to interrupt any more of his naps
and to be a faithful traveling companion.

Most importantly,
she promised to remember that her story was really *their* story,
that it had been shared with her as a gift,
and that she should never pretend it was hers alone.
And as long as she did that
she would never *be* alone
because the story belonged to both of them.

But now that the story has been shared
and its deepest soul exposed,
It doesn't just belong to the two of them any longer.

It belongs to all of us.

ACKNOWLEDGMENTS

If you've made it this far (and are even reading the acknowledgments—go you!!), I owe you, my reader, an incredible debt of thanks. This is my first book, and without the hope that readers like you are out there, I could never have created it. With love and honor for you on your journey, wherever it may lead, thank you. I would also like to thank my mother, Janice, sister, Maureen, and my friends Lisa and Maggie (the same Maggie whose art adorns the cover of this book), for putting up with my many requests for feedback with unending patience. A shout out to my cheerleaders, April, Kim, and Suzanne, who were always ready to pep me up with support and encouragement as I faced my fears of putting my words out into the world. Thank you to my developmental editor, Julia Pastore, for her thoughtful questions that pushed me to clarify key material in the text. And I am grateful for the cheerful affability with which my Bublish team, Shilah LaCoe and Katherine Meiss, accommodated my many questions and schedule tweaks. I'm appreciative, too, for the assistance of the rest of my editing team; each one of you left the book better than you found it and has contributed to making the finished work what it is today.

A special note of gratitude to my line editor, AL. Your heartfelt message meant so much to me I printed it, cut it out, and put it on my home altar.

My thoughts and prayers are with you. When I hear from readers who don't resonate with my work, as is inevitable in life, I will never forget that my words had a powerful positive impact on someone I did not know. Truly, it makes the hours of love I poured into this book worth it. Thank you from the bottom of *my* heart.

Made in the USA
Monee, IL
03 March 2022

92239885R00144